INTRODUCTION

Several years ago as I was leaving Washington after giving a course of demonstration lectures in hygienic cookery, I was impressed with the thought that a cook book (which my friends had been urging me to write) giving the results of my experience, would be the means of reaching the greatest number of people with knowledge on health subjects.

As a result of that thought, this book comes with earnest, heartfelt greeting to all other works of the same nature, not as a rival but as a co-worker in the great plan of glorifying our Creator. 1 Cor. 10:31.

In its preparation, I have purposed to make the book practical, avoiding technicalities and to some extent conventionalities, and have endeavored to "meet the people where they are" by not being extreme or radical; and at the same time to make principles of truth so clear that many will be won from "the indulgence of appetite, which places them in such a condition of health that there is a constant warring against the soul's highest interests."

While there are recipes especially for those who entertain, there is an abundant variety of directions for carefully prepared simple dishes.

The explicit general directions will not be needed by all, but from my twenty years of experience in teaching, I know that many will value them.

The foods richest in proteids are classed as "True Meats" and no flesh meat names are used in the book.

This collection contains the choicest of those of my recipes which have been published by others in various books and periodicals at different times.

I am indebted to an innumerable company of people of all classes for *ideas*, for which I would be glad to thank each one personally if it were possible.

Though there is hardly any choice, the recipes marked with a star are especially practical and desirable.

All unnamed quotations are from "The Ministry of Healing" or other works by the same author.

That "The Laurel Health Cookery" may bring rich blessings to many households is my earnest prayer.

CONTENTS

INTRODUCTION
GENERAL
    Cooking Utensils, their Uses and Care
    Things to Do Beforehand
    Economy
    Miscellaneous
    Measurements
    Flavorings
    Garnishings
FRUITS
    Fresh
    Cooked
    To Can
    Jellies
    Jams
TO CAN VEGETABLES
TO DRY VEGETABLES
SOUPS
    Suggestions
    Water Soups
    Cream and Milk Soups
    Bisques
    Chowders
    Purees
    Our Famous Soups
    Fruit Soups
    Soup Garnishes and Accompaniments

GENERAL

COOKING UTENSILS, THEIR USES AND CARE

"A good housekeeper without perfected kitchen conveniences is as much of an anomaly as a carpenter without a plane, a dressmaker without a sewing machine."—*Anonym.*

What would we think of the farmer who to-day was cutting his hay with a scythe and reaping his grain with a cradle because he could not "afford" a reaper and mower?

While we should be able to adapt ourselves to circumstances, to improvise double boilers, steamers and ovens when necessary, it is at the same time true economy to have an abundance of cooking utensils if possible. A half dozen saucepans will last six times as long as one used for everything and save much valuable time.

"To many people, anything out of the usual custom is deemed extravagant." This I suppose accounts for the fact that many housewives who have beautifully furnished parlors and wear fine clothing cannot afford conveniences for the kitchen.

The room in which is prepared the "food to sustain life and nourish brain, bone and muscle," should be the most attractive place in the house, and it will be when arranged and furnished for convenience. I can think of nothing more interesting than a kitchen with the frequently used utensils decorating the walls where they can be reached with few steps; and such little things as spoons, egg beaters, can openers, spatulas, cork screws, potato mashers, measuring cups, funnels, soup dippers, wire strainers, pinchers and skimmers, not forgetting a small cushion with pins, hanging just over the table; the table having drawers for knives, vegetable cutters and other unhangable articles.

The best quality of aluminum ware is the cheapest and best for fruits and for general cooking purposes, except for vegetables.

Never put lye or anything alkaline into aluminum vessels.

Copper and re-tinned vessels are unequaled in some respects (if they may not be used for acid foods); being flat bottomed, thick and heavy, milk, legumes, cereals and foods of that nature are not so apt to stick or scorch in them, and they are almost everlasting. They can be re-tinned when the lining wears off.

Iron kettles and frying pans are excellent for many things. Some of the uses of a nice smooth iron frying pan are to bake a round cake or a thick pie or a pudding in, to scallop corn or potatoes, or to scald milk.

Use granite, agate, and porcelain lined utensils with care.

Never dry them on the stove as that causes them to crack; and do not knock the edges of the kettles and saucepans with a spoon, nor strike any kind of a vessel with an agate spoon, as it causes the little particles of glazing to flake off. These flakes from agate utensils often work serious injury to the delicate membranes of the digestive tract.

One large double boiler holding from 8 to 16 qts. is very desirable as it furnishes two kettles for fruit canning and other purposes and can be used as a double boiler when required. Several smaller ones of different sizes economize time and food material.

To improvise a double boiler, set a close covered pan over a kettle of boiling water; or set a covered dish into a pail with water in it, cover and put into the oven; or put a pan or other covered vessel into a kettle of water on top of the stove with something under it to keep it from the bottom of the kettle; or set one milk crock into another, with water in the lower one; or a bowl into the top of the teakettle. The first double boiler I ever owned was a gluepot.

Use wire strainers or small and large colanders, well covered, over dishes of boiling water, for steamers; and when a deeper receptacle is required, turn a basin or pan that just fits, over the top.

Two sizes of flat colanders with pin head holes are to be found at the 5 and 10 cent stores, which are just as useful and durable as more expensive ones. They answer the purpose of both steamer and colander.

Be sure to have deep kettles or boilers into which the colanders fit perfectly. I have been in kitchens where, though there was a sufficient variety of utensils, they were of little use, for no two things fitted; the steamers and colanders were just a little too large or a little too small for all the kettles, requiring double the expenditure of time and strength in using.

Iron rings from small wooden kegs or little rings melted from the tops of tin cans are great treasures to use on the top of the stove, in kettles, or in the oven, to set vessels on to keep the contents from sticking and burning.

"Gunboats"—empty tin cans—of all sizes, have a great variety of uses.

A book of asbestos sheets costing ten cents is invaluable. Each sheet can be used again and again for laying over bread, cake and other foods in the oven.

After using an aluminum frying or omelet pan for a time, one would always feel it to be a necessity.

The uses of timbale molds and custard cups are almost innumerable, and when you once get them you have them.

A pastry brush saves greasy fingers and much time, in oiling cold or warm pans. Never use it on a *hot* griddle.

For dispatch and thoroughness in oiling round bottomed gem pans, nothing equals a piece of cloth folded in several thicknesses 2½ to 3 in.

square, saturated with oil.

A spatula (similar to a palette knife) of medium size will soon pay for itself in the material it saves from the sides of the pans, as well as in time.

A large French knife chops vegetables on a board more rapidly than they can be done in a chopping bowl; it also slices onions, shaves cabbage, cuts croutons and does many things as no other knife can, while smaller ones of different sizes all have their uses.

For stirring dry flour and meal into hot liquid, for gravies, and for beating all batters, nothing can take the place of a strong wire batter whip.

The "Surprise" beater with fine cross wires makes the whites of eggs for meringues and cakes lighter than any other. The smaller the wire around the edge, the lighter the eggs will be. These very delicate ones are for sale in some of the five and ten cent stores at 3 for 5c. Next to the "Surprise" beater for beating whites of eggs comes the silver fork.

The "Dover" revolving beater gives a fine close grain when that is desired, as in egg creams, the "Holt" coming next and being more rapid in its work, while the "Lyon" gives a fine, fluffy result. A large sized beater is more useful.

Eggs can be beaten in a deep bowl, narrow at the bottom (the regular cooking bowl shape) in half the time that it takes to beat them in a broad bottomed bowl. The nearer the sides of the bowl are to the beater, the quicker the work will be done. The same is true of whipping cream, and as cream spatters at first, a pitcher or a tin can, not so deep but the handle of the beater can be operated, is best for the purpose. It is better to set the dish in the sink while whipping cream.

If possible have a good scale, as much more accurate results are obtained in cooking by weight than by measure. It will be useful in weighing articles from the grocery and market, for weighing letters and papers for mailing and many other things.

When you have used a good bread mixer for a time, you would not go back to the old, laborious way of kneading bread for double its cost. The mixer also makes better bread than can be made by hand.

PUDDING MOLDS
COPPER SAUCE PAN
TURK'S HEAD MOLD
BORDER MOLD
ALUMINUM OMELET PAN
SURPRISE BEATER

One of the greatest labor savers is a food cutter. A large sized one, even for a small family, is most satisfactory. Many now have a nut butter attachment which is desirable, though a regular nut butter mill is preferable for nut preparations.

Try to have something for a quick fire. If you are out of the reach of gas, a well-cared-for two burner oil stove will do good service.

Eternal vigilance is the price of preventing double boilers from going dry. Add more water before there is the least danger.

Rinse off the egg beater or batter whip and hang it in its place as soon as you finish using it, before going on with what you are doing, unless, as in some cakes, it needs to drain, then have ready a pitcher, tin can or quart measure containing cold water to drop it into after draining.

The cogs of an egg beater should never be wet; when they are wet once, its usefulness is impaired.

The "Surprise" beater should never be touched with a cloth.

Always wipe a can opener after using, and hang it in its place.

Wire strainers should always be rinsed as soon as used; colanders also, unless they require soaking, in which case put them immediately into water.

Put sticky utensils to soaking as soon as emptied.

Rinse and put to draining everything that can be rinsed; then it will be ready for use instead of rusting in the sink.

Never put knives, spatulas, egg beaters or whips in the sink; always rinse them off at once.

Professional cooks never lay a knife down without wiping it off. Clean, dry cloths or towels should be at hand for such purposes.

A side towel fastened to the waist is almost a necessity.

Never scrape a knife or spoon on the edge of a dish.

It is just as necessary and as satisfactory to keep the inside of the oven blackened as the top of the stove, and it is very little more work.

Boil strong lye water in a scorched vessel (except aluminum), before trying to clean it.

I have noticed that if a little water is boiled for a few minutes in a close covered vessel in which some pasty food has been cooked, the particles are so loosened by the steam that the vessel washes easily.

I would suggest that instead of hanging the dish cloth on the inside of the sink door, you put it on a line near the stove or out of doors, where it will dry quickly.

Wet wooden spoons, chopping bowls and all wooden utensils in cold water before using, to prevent their absorbing the flavors and juices of foods.

Put new bread and cake tins into a hot oven and bake them until they look like old ones, if you wish your bread and cake to be well done on the bottom and sides.

Do not work in a "mess," keep your tables wiped up as you go.

Above all, *pick up after yourself.* It is often more work to pick up after people than to do the work.

THINGS TO DO BEFOREHAND

Wash potatoes and keep in stone crock in cool place.

Have beans, peas and lentils looked over.

Have English currants washed and dried, in jars.

Have seeded raisins stemmed.

Have peanuts and almonds blanched.

Have herbs and flavorings ground and bottled.

Have citron cut, wrapped in waxed paper, in covered jar.

Have flour browned in three shades.

Have dry bread ground.

Have tomatoes strained.

Have lemon juice extracted, standing in a cool place.

ECONOMY

"Gather up the fragments that remain that nothing be lost." John 6:13.

True economy consists in using all of a good material, rather than in buying an inferior quality.

It is poor economy from a financial standpoint (saying nothing of health) to buy small or specked fruits or vegetables.

It takes longer to pare, quarter and core a specked apple than a sound one, because the decayed part has first to be cut out and one may have to cut again and again before it is all removed and when it is finished there may not remain a quarter of an apple.

I once saw two barrels of apples bought at a great "bargain." Four or five people whose time was valuable spent an afternoon in preparing those apples to stew; when they had finished, there was just a bushel left and they were so flavorless that it was necessary to add lemon juice and a good deal of sugar to make them at all palatable.

C. F. Langworthy, Ph. D. in speaking of overripe and partially decayed fruit says: "In addition to a deterioration in flavor, there is always the possibility of digestive disturbance if such fruit is eaten raw."—*Farmers' Bulletin 293. U. S. Department of Agriculture.*

Inferior, immature fruit, dried, requires a larger proportion of sugar than well ripened fruit, and then it is neither palatable nor wholesome.

Small prunes with their large proportion of stone and skin are expensive besides being inferior in flavor.

It takes as long to pare, quarter and core a small apple as a large one, and a bushel of large apples will yield more pulp than a bushel of small ones, notwithstanding the spaces, there being a so much larger proportion of skins and cores in the small ones.

Small pineapples are especially expensive.

"Cheap" flour costs more than the best because it takes a larger quantity to make the same amount of bread.

Corn starch that costs two or three cents less per package than the best will sometimes require double the quantity for thickening, besides imparting a strong, disagreeable flavor.

Cotton seed oil that is not well refined, so that it is clear and nearly white is not fit for food, and requires more for shortening.

Economy in all things, food, clothing, houses, climate is that which keeps us in the best condition physically and spiritually.

MISCELLANEOUS

All foods that are suitable should be used uncooked. They are more nourishing and consequently more satisfying.

Foods containing starch should not be eaten raw.

Next to wholesomeness, make taste and palatability first. There is nothing more disappointing than to taste of a daintily arranged and decorated dish and find it flat and insipid.

Seek to develop the natural flavors of foods, of which there are thousands, rather than to add foreign flavorings.

To stir fruits, legumes and many foods while cooking is just the way to make them stick and scorch. Shake the vessels instead of stirring.

To brush kettles and saucepans on the inside with oil, helps to keep milk and other foods from sticking.

Use double boilers as far as possible for reheating gravies, cereals and legumes, and for heating milk.

When, in spite of all precautions, something burns on, plunge the vessel without ceremony into a pail or pan of cold water for a moment, empty the contents immediately into another kettle, add boiling water and return to the fire to finish cooking. Badly scorched foods often lose all the scorched flavor by this treatment.

Remove the burnt portion from bread or cake with a grater, when first taken from the oven.

Dip the knife into hot water to cut butter, warm bread or cake.

Two forks are better than a knife for separating steamed puddings, fresh cake and many things.

Use pastry flour for gravies, sauces and all thickenings.

To blend flour and liquid for thickening, add only a little liquid at a time, stirring with a fork or batter whip until a perfectly smooth paste is formed, then add liquid to make of the consistency of rather thin cream.

Flour, for thickening, gives a more creamy consistency than corn starch. Use corn starch for fruit juices, as it leaves them clearer.

Never mix flour or corn starch with eggs to stir into boiling liquid, as they both require longer cooking than eggs will bear without separating. Stir the blended flour or corn starch into the liquid first, let it boil well, then pour the hot mixture gradually, stirring, into the beaten eggs, return to the fire and cook a moment if necessary, but do not boil.

In adding yolks of eggs to hot mixtures, put two or three spoonfuls of the mixture on to the yolks, stirring, then add them, all at once, to the whole.

Eggs must be added all at once to hot liquids so they will all be cooked alike and a part will not curdle before the rest is done.

To prevent a raw taste, blended flour should be added to boiling liquid so slowly as not to stop its boiling.

"Rich milk" means one-fourth to one-third cream.

Cream judiciously used is no more expensive from a financial stand point than butter, and from a health standpoint it is cheaper.

Being in the form of an emulsion, cream does not hinder digestion as does the free fat of butter. It should be sterilized before using in uncooked dishes.

In the recipes in this book, heavy cream is meant unless thin is specified.

It is cheaper to buy heavy cream than light, when there are two qualities, and you can make it as thin as you wish.

When cream is scarce do not use it where oil and skimmed milk will do just as well, but save it for uses where nothing else will take its place.

Cream with water often gives a better flavor to foods than milk, and is just as cheap.

For farmers, the use of cream saves the labor of making butter.

When taking cream, use fewer nuts and less butter and other oils.

Nut creams and butters may always be substituted for dairy cream and butter, with judgment as to flavors.

Peanut butter should be used sparingly and judiciously. No one enjoys, as one man expressed it, "that everlasting peanut flavor in everything."

Oil and melted butter may be combined in equal quantities when the butter flavor is desirable, as in pilau and drawn butter.

Oil makes more tender pastry, raised cakes and universal crust.

"Stale" bread crumbs are those of a two or three days old loaf.

Stale bread is understood for crumbs when no specification is given.

A quick and easy way to prepare stale bread crumbs is to cut very thin slices from the loaf, lay them together and cut as thin as possible across one way and then the other with a large sharp knife into tiny dice.

"Dry" crumbs are those from a loaf dry enough to grate or grind.

Save all pieces of bread not usable for croutons or other things, dry without browning, and roll or grind, for dry crumbs; sift, leaving two sizes of crumbs.

When bread crumbs are used for puddings or molds the quantity will vary with the kind of bread. Fewer will be required with home-made bread than with baker's bread.

Bread, cracker or zwieback crumbs, corn meal, flour or browned flour No. 1, or a mixture of crumbs and brown or white flour may be used for rolling croquettes or cutlets, or for sprinkling the top of scallops or gratins.

Nut meal is suitable for the outside of rice croquettes and the top of many dishes.

Grated or chopped onion is apt to become bitter if prepared long before using.

To extract the juice from lemons without a drill, cut them in halves without rolling, the same as for a drill, then holding each half over a strainer in a bowl, work the point of a spoon from the cut surface in and around gradually to the rind. This method removes the juice cleaner than does the drill.

Another way is to roll the lemon and puncture it at one end with a silver fork, then squeeze the juice out. This leaves the seeds inside.

Dry lemons yield more juice than fresh ones.

Remove the pulp from lemons for pies and other uses by cutting them lengthwise in the middle of the sections and scraping each side of the membrane, or by cutting the lemon in halves crosswise and taking the pulp out with a spoon.

To keep lemons and oranges from molding, spread them on a shelf in a dry place so that they will not touch each other. They may be covered with glass tumblers if in a cool as well as dry place.

To core apples, insert a steel fork at the blossom end and turn it round and round, then repeat from the stem end.

The half shell of an egg will remove bits of shell from broken eggs much better than a spoon.

My mother taught me to use too little rather than too much salt in foods, saying it was easier to add it than to take it out.

Salt varies so much in saltness that it is impossible to give definite rules for its use.

Have a shelf over the stove for zwieback, crackers and toasted cereals to keep them crisp.

Keep a dish of oil on or near your work table.

Have a small tin of pastry flour on the table to use for thickening sauces; also a small bowl or tin of sugar, and one of corn starch if using it frequently, and a box of salt, of course.

If a thickened mixture is allowed to any more than boil up well, after lemon juice is added, it will become thin.

Finely-sliced, tender, raw celery is much to be preferred to cooked, in timbales, croquettes, batters and sauces.

Never chop celery; slice it fine instead.

The word "meat" as used in this book refers to true meats, not flesh meats, but is confined to such foods as are rich in proteids, not being taken in its broadest sense.

Use soft butter for oiling molds to be decorated, as that holds the decorations better than oil.

To unmold, dip the mold in hot water a moment.

Both oil and crumb molds for delicate fillings.

Dip molds in cold water, invert and turn quickly right side up without draining, for gelatine and other fillings to be served cold.

Many foods gain in richness of flavor by being reheated; and for that reason, left overs often make more appetizing dishes than fresh cooked foods.

Reheat foods, legumes, vegetables, cereals, or fruits, to preserve them, before they begin to show signs of spoiling.

Only a small quantity of sugar, proportionately, should be added to yolks of eggs, or they will gather in small, hard particles and become useless.

Ice water crisps and freshens such vegetables as lettuce, parsley, cabbage and cucumbers as that just a little warmer will not.

In multiplying a recipe to make a larger quantity of soup or other liquid food, use a smaller proportion of liquid; or in dishes containing thickening take a larger proportion of flour, as the evaporation is not so great in proportion to the quantity.

The alcohol of yeast or of flavoring extracts goes off in the steam in cooking.

When eggs are used in cakes, breads, puddings or other dishes, fewer nuts, nut foods, legumes or other proteid foods will be required.

Bake soufflés and dishes made light with eggs, slowly, as when baked rapidly they puff up quickly and fall just as quickly; while if baked slowly, they retain their lightness.

Timbales, puddings and all molds to be served hot should stand 5 or 10 m. in a warm place after removing from the fire, before unmolding.

Place a cold wet towel over pudding molds to loosen, if inclined to stick.

Do not chop nut meats fine for roasts, cakes or puddings. Sometimes leave them whole, or just break them a little.

To try vegetables for tenderness, use a sharp pointed knife rather than a fork.

Batter and plum puddings and brown bread may be steamed in the oven by setting the mold containing them into a vessel of water with a tight fitting cover.

To steam in glass, set dishes or jars first into cold water and bring to boiling, then set into steamer.

Honey attracts moisture, consequently it should be kept in a warm dry place.

In discarding unwholesome foods be sure to put something wholesome in their place; in other words, employ a system of substitution rather than one of subtraction.

For instance, for this book we have taken pains to search out a variety of harmless flavorings to be used in place of the irritating condiments, such as mustard, pepper, ginger, cinnamon, nutmeg and cloves; and instead of the acetic acid of vinegar, we use lemon juice—citric acid.

"Vinegar—acetic acid, is about ten times as strong as alcohol and makes more trouble in the stomach than any of the other acids except oxalic."—*Dr. Rand.*

"Do not eat largely of salt."

"Very hot food ought not to be taken into the stomach. Soups, puddings and other articles of the kind are often eaten too hot, and as a consequence the stomach is debilitated."

Many people can digest cream better when accompanied by an acid fruit.

While using oil enough to keep the machinery of the body lubricated, take care not to use too much. People with dilated stomachs can take very little, and that little best in salad dressings or as shortening with flour.

Malt gives flesh but not strength; too much is harmful.

Flesh is more often a sign of disease than of health. Good solid firm muscle is to be cultivated.

Taste is a matter of education. Let us educate ourselves to like the things that are good for us.

"Perseverance in a self-denying course of eating and drinking will soon make plain, wholesome food palatable, and it will be eaten with greater satisfaction than the epicure enjoys over his rich dainties."

MEASUREMENTS

Flour is always sifted once before measuring and is laid into the measure lightly with a spoon to just level, without being shaken down; when measured otherwise, results will not be correct.

The measurements of tablespoons and teaspoons in this book are for slightly rounded spoons, as granulated sugar would be when the spoon is shaken sidewise. This seems the natural way of measuring. When level spoons are specified, the spoon is leveled off with a spatula or the straight edge of a knife.

The half-pint cup is the standard measuring cup.

A cupful is all the cup will hold without running over.

A speck	equals ¼ saltspn.
1 saltspn	equals ¼ teaspn.
2 teaspns	equals 1 dessert spn.
1½ dessert spn	equals 1 tablespn.
3 teaspns	equals 1 tablespn.
1 tablespn. sugar or corn starch	equals 1½ level tablespn.
3 level tablespns. cracker crumbs	equals ¼ cup.
9½ tablespns. granulated sugar	equals 1 cup.
15¼ level tablespns. granulated sugar	equals 1 cup.
3 tablespns. liquid	equals ¼ cup.
4 tablespns. liquid	equals ⅓ cup.
4½ level tablespns. butter	equals ⅓ cup.

3 rounded tablespns. butter	equals ⅓ cup.
12 tablespns. liquid	equals 1 cup.
1 wine glass	equals ¼ cup.
1 gill	equals ½ cup.
1 cup	equals ½ pint.
1 tumbler	equals ½ pint.
4 gills–2 cups	equals 1 pint.
2 pints	equals 1 quart.
4 quarts	equals 1 gallon.
2 cups (1 pint) granulated sugar	equals 1 pound.
2½ cups powdered sugar	equals 1 pound.
3⅔ cups light or medium brown sugar	equals 1 pound
2 cups butter	equals 1 pound
4 cups good pastry flour	equals 1 pound
3½–3⅞ cups good bread flour	equals 1 pound
3½ plus, cups rice	equals 1 pound
3 cups seeded raisins	equals 1 pound
3¼ cups currants	equals 1 pound
4 cups desiccated cocoanut	equals 1 pound
1 pint milk or water	equals 1 pound
1 rounded tablespn. butter	equals 1 ounce
Butter size of a walnut	equals 1 ounce
Butter size of an egg	equals 2 ounces
2 tablespns. oil	equals 1⅛ ounce
1 cup of oil	equals 6¾ ounces
2 rounded tablespns. flour	equals 1 ounce
1 rounded tablespn. sugar	equals 1 ounce
1½ level tablespn. table salt	equals 1 ounce
8 eggs in shell	equals 1 pound
10 eggs out of shell	equals 1 pound
12 ears of corn	equals 3 cups grated corn
1 ear of corn	equals ¼ cup grated corn
18 roots of oyster plant	equals 1¼ qt. sliced
1 bunch of oyster plant	equals ⅔ qt. sliced

1 bunch of oyster plant   equals 1 pt. after cooking

FLAVORINGS

If we heed the injunction of the wise man to eat for strength and not for drunkenness, we will exclude the burning, irritating condiments from our dietary, since they by causing a feverish state of the system and creating "a thirst which water cannot quench," are among the greatest causes of inebriety.

When our sense of taste is not benumbed or destroyed by harmful accompaniments we are in a condition to keenly enjoy the thousands of fine, delicate flavors that our loving Father has placed in wholesome foods.

Among the stronger flavors for those who do not at once enjoy the delicate ones, we have sage, savory, thyme, marjoram, rosemary, bay leaf, garlic, onion, chives and leeks.

Then come celery salt and seed, leaves and stalks; lemon thyme, shallots, spearmint, parsley, basil and tarragon.

The flavors of carrots, turnips, cabbage and spinach have their place.

The small leaf buds of sassafras may be dried and ground for soups and stews.

Celery leaves dried with gentle heat make excellent flavorings. They may be powdered by rubbing through a wire strainer the same as leaf sage.

Crush stalks of celery and let them stand in the soup or sauce to be flavored for 15 m., then remove them.

For a fresh positive onion flavor, let slices of onion stand in the food for 5 or 10 m.

The flavor of garlic is usually obtained by rubbing the dish in which the food is to be served or the spoon with which it is stirred with the cut surface of one of the cloves or sections. Slice it and crush it with salt when using it in cooked foods. One clove will flavor a large quantity.

Use bay leaf in the proportion of one large leaf to a quart of liquid.

As far as possible raise your own herbs. If in no other way, plant them in pots and boxes in the house. Somewhere I have seen the suggestion of planting parsley in holes in the sides of a barrel which has been sawed in two, and such plants as sage, thyme, mint, basil and tarragon in the top.

Gather herbs before flowering, dry in the shade, tie in paper sacks and hang in a dry place. Powder only a small quantity at a time and keep in close covered small jars. Fresh herbs, especially mint and tarragon, when obtainable, are far superior to dry ones.

The fact that raising any oil to a temperature high enough to brown it, decomposes it and produces a poisonous acid—a powerful irritant—is one of the best known to science.

Flour is rendered more digestible by browning and when combined with cream, oil or butter, gives the browned oil flavor without the poison.

To prepare browned flour, sift *bread* flour into a broad flat pan, let it stand in a warm oven, stirring occasionally, until thoroughly dry, then gradually increase the heat of the oven, stirring often, until the desired degree of brownness is reached.

A delicate cream color, so light that you would hardly know there was any color except by comparing it with flour that had not been in the oven, gives a delightfully meaty flavor to some gravies and sauces. A light or medium brown is convenient to have at times, but the one most useful is the dark chestnut brown. The darker it is the longer it will last, as less of it will be required for flavoring.

To obtain this color a very high degree of heat will be required at the last, with almost constant stirring. As this dark flour lasts so long (I seldom make it more than once in a year for a large family), it pays to give it the necessary attention at every stage. Do not try to hurry it. If you begin browning it before it is thoroughly dry, it will burn. When done, sift and keep in close covered can or jar.

The lightest shade (which for convenience we call No. 1, and the others No. 2 and 3) should be prepared oftener as it becomes stale by standing. No. 3 will keep indefinitely. It is used for flavoring only as it will not thicken. Where consistency is desired, combine it with unbrowned flour. No. 1 will thicken nearly as much as though it had not been in the oven, and No. 2 a little.

When no number is given in recipes calling for browned flour, No. 3 is understood.

Browned flour, onion and a small quantity of tomato (not enough to give a tomato taste) combined, form the basis of meaty flavors in foods.

To these, add sometimes a bay leaf, a very little sage and a trifle of thyme. Again, add bay leaf, grated or chopped carrot and a very few celery tops, dried or fresh.

Garlic combines well with either of these combinations, and powdered or soaked dried mushrooms are a delightful addition.

Butter (oil or part oil) and a little onion with parsley seem something like chicken.

Juniper berries are thought to give the flavor of game. Not more than a teaspoonful of crushed berries should be used to the quart of stew.

Combine flavors so that no one is prominent but the whole combination pleasing.

Use herbs and all strong flavorings sparingly. One colored cook of experience expressed it when she said, "I put in just a trifle of sage, not enough to make it vulgar."

For sauces, soups and croquettes.

Cook together sliced onions, browned flour and oil with salt and water until onions are tender; strain, keep in cool place.

FOR SWEETS

Steep peach leaves in water for almond flavor.

Finely-ground coriander seed is a delightful and not unwholesome flavoring. It is cheaper to buy the seed by the pound. A half pound will go a long way. Do not grind too much at a time.

Ground anise seed in minute quantities is unequaled for some things, but is disagreeable when used too liberally.

For sweet dishes to be flavored with lemon or orange, score the rind of the fruit lightly with a sharp-tined fork. Drop the scored fruit into the measured sugar and rub it well with the sugar.

Another way of obtaining the flavor, also of grape fruit, is to pour boiling water over the thinly-pared yellow rind and when cold, strain. For salads, let that thin rind stand in the lemon or other fruit juices for a time and then remove.

When obliged to use lemon or orange extracts, use only a few drops instead of the teaspoonful of the average recipe.

Rose is another of the delightful flavors to be used sparingly.

To flavor with cocoanut, when the fibre is not desired, steep (do not boil) the cocoanut in milk for 15–20 m., then strain it out.

SALAD FLAVORINGS

To flavor lemon juice for cooked or uncooked dressings, take to each three tablespns. of lemon juice and one of water, a slice of onion, a bay leaf, and

¼ teaspn. of celery seed or 1 tablespn. of chopped celery leaves. Boil a moment, then cool and strain. Tarragon and chives may be used for the flavorings. Onion, bay leaf, thyme, a trifle of garlic if liked, and a few thin yellow-slices of orange peel make another combination.

The salad dish is sometimes rubbed with the cut surface of a clove of garlic or a slice of onion, or onion may be chopped or grated. Crushed celery seed is liked by some in salad dressings. Spearmint is very refreshing. Delicate tender sassafras leaves may be used in fruit and nut meat salads.

Shredded fresh mint combines well with orange or grape fruit or with currant juice; tarragon with red raspberries and currants, and basil with peaches.

In closing the subject of flavorings, I quote the words of a lady visitor after sampling some of the dishes prepared by a class in cookery:

"Any one can give a taste to foods by adding condiments and flavorings, but to develop the flavors of the foods themselves is an art."

GARNISHING

The saying that "some people eat with their eyes" is true to a great extent of all of us. I believe that the veriest savage would better enjoy his dinner, however rude, if somewhere there were tucked into it a bit of green. The busy farmer's wife as she goes to the wood pile for an armful of wood can quickly pick off a spray of May weed, dropping it into a tin of cold water as she passes the water pail, and her platter of beans for dinner is transformed, in the eyes of those children, into a thing of beauty, and what effect may it not have in the formation of their characters?

Of variety in garnishing there need be no lack with the garden, wayside and woods abounding in beautiful leaves, vines and flowers.

There are foliage plant, geranium, and autumn leaves, ferns in variety, with lettuce, endive, spinach, parsley, chervil and carrot tops. The variegated variety of beet leaves, as also the bright blossoms of nasturtiums make a brilliant garnish.

Put parsley, ferns, and all of the green leaves and vines into very cold water as soon as gathered and leave for some time, then keep in paper sacks in a cold place away from the wind. Repeat the cold water bath at intervals.

Barberries canned, or preserved in brine, candied cranberries or cherries, green grapes in brine, designs cut from orange, lemon grape fruit and tangerine rinds, tomatoes in slices or in lengthwise pieces, and slices of lemon or orange with the skin on are all suitable garnishes at times.

Lemon cups, having a slice cut off from the ends so that they will stand, may be used for mayonnaise or small servings of salad.

Orange and grape fruit halves with tops notched or scalloped or sometimes cut in deep points rolled down, and orange baskets make a change of service. All of these fruit cups should be kept in ice water or chopped ice until serving time, then thoroughly dried with a soft towel.

Blood oranges and gelatine oranges are novelties for garnishing.

Sprays of maidenhair fern are pretty under grape fruit and orange cups.

All cups or glasses containing salads or creams should be served on doilies on small plates.

To prepare fringed celery, cut the stalks into two- or three-in. lengths, then slice very fine from each end to within ¾–1 in. of the center and leave in ice water for a time. Do not lay in ice water before preparing. The short tender stalks may have the leaves left on and be shredded at the opposite end. Celery *leaves* make a desirable garnish.

Cut carrots, beets and yellow turnips into slices or sticks, or into round pieces with an open-top thimble or a round pastry tube, and into fancy shapes with vegetable cutters, selecting cutters which have not sharp points or slender stems.

Radish Lilies

Get either the turnip or olive shaped radishes, wash them well, trim off just the slender tips and all but one or two of the smallest leaves. With a thin, sharp knife cut them into halves from the tip end almost to the stem, and the same way into quarters and eighths. Then carefully loosen the rind of each section as far down as it is cut and throw the radishes into ice water, leaving them there for several hours or overnight, when they will have bloomed into beautiful lilies. Pure white or yellow lilies may be made from yellow or white radishes. Serve directly from the ice water, and the radishes will be crisp and sweet and easily digested.

Just one radish sometimes, in a spray or two of parsley or chervil is better than a more elaborate garnish; a red radish sliced or cut into quarters or sixths is pretty in a little green.

Roll up imperfect leaves of lettuce and slice in thin slices, then pick up lightly and use for borders or nests or beds.

Dry parsley thoroughly in a towel before chopping. For rolling, spread the particles out, a little distance apart, so as to just fleck whatever is rolled in it.

Use nuts chopped or in halves or broken pieces for borders or nests of fruit or vegetable salads; never put them into the dressing.

Potato Balls

Potatoes may be cut into balls with a vegetable scoop, boiled until just tender, not broken, drained, sprinkled with chopped parsley and used for garnishing a true meat dish.

Egg Daisies

Cut the hard boiled yolks of eggs into round pieces and the whites into petal shapes for daisies for decorating the tops of small spinach or other timbales or molds.

The whites and yolks are better poached separately for garnishing. Cut whites with vegetable cutters sometimes.

Oxeye Daisies

Use the end of a small black olive for the center of daisies, and carrots for the leaves.

Toast points or croutons of different shapes are suitable garnishes for timbales, eggs, broiled mushrooms and true meat or vegetable stews, or we may use pieces of bread of different shapes that have been dipped in egg yolks and milk and baked. Breaded triangles, squares or circles, of corn meal porridge may be used to garnish the edge of a platter for a stew.

Serve some creamed dishes or stews in shells of pastry.

Turk's head and border molds may be decorated with truffles or other decorations, and used for meat dishes for variety.

Button mushrooms may be used for garnishing individual timbales.

Cut left overs of pie crust or cracker dough into fancy shapes, for scalloped dishes, salads and some desserts, and into squares, diamonds or strips for peas and other vegetables.

For legumes or other meat dishes, sometimes use carrots in dice or slices, sprinkled with chopped parsley or interspersed with sprigs of parsley.

Lemon Points.—Cut slices of lemon into four or six parts.

Pastry Bag

The pastry bag gives variety in garnishing and decorating. The bag itself may be of rubber, paper or cloth. Cloth for all purposes is the most practical. To make, take "Indian Head" or other heavy cloth, cut it into any sized square desired; fold and sew together in cornucopia shape (the seam is better felled), trim the top evenly and hem; then cut off a very little from the point and hem that, leaving the opening just large enough to insert the tubes one-third to one-half their length.

Paper bags may be used in an emergency, and rubber for some purposes, but not for anything containing oil.

Mashed peas and potatoes should not be too dry for decorating.

Mayonnaise dressing and whipped cream should be stiff, as also meringues.

COLORINGS

Pokeberry—Carmine

Cover berries with water, boil till the skins break, strain, add 1 cup of sugar to each pint of juice; boil, bottle, seal.

For Red, cook strained tomato to a thick pulp; or slice a bright red raw beet into cold water and let it stand on the stove where it will heat slowly to a little below the boiling point and strain.

For Green, bruise parsley, spinach, chervil, onion tops, chives, tarragon or lettuce, with or without lemon, and press out the juice for coloring.

For Yellow, steep saffron in boiling water for ½–1 hour and strain when cold.

When these colorings are not suitable, the so-called "fruit colors" for sale at the groceries may be used. Use only enough for delicate shades.

ARRANGEMENT AND GARNISHING OF SALADS

The arrangement and garnishing of salads depends largely upon individual taste and skill in the use of things at hand, and is a matter of importance.

The garnish should be a suitable one and should harmonize with the ingredients of the salad. For example, a dainty flower or vine with a delicate fruit salad, and slices or fancy shapes of vegetables with true meat salads.

Red apple, or tomato cups may be used for light colored salads, and yellow tomato, or green and white apple cups for bright ones.

Juicy fruit salads should be served in dainty glasses or cups; and a correspondingly dainty doily on the plate underneath the glass with a delicate flower or leaf by its side, leaves nothing to be desired.

"We do not attain perfection by striving to do something out of the common.
"Perfection is acquired by doing the common things uncommonly well."—*Mowry.*

FRUITS

FRUITS—FRESH

"Man has always thrived as he has eaten freely of fruits."—*H. Irving Hancock.*

"The best food on this planet is ripe fruit. The healthiest people on the globe are the fruit eaters of tropical countries. The great muscular Maoris of New Zealand are a frugiverous race. I have seen a boat crew of these great chocolate colored giants that would outrow the 'crack' university crews were they properly trained. The bread fruit of the Samoan Islands has made a race of giants. I have examined these men and women on their native soil and finer human specimens never lived."—*Dr. Paul Edwards.*

"The more we depend upon the fresh fruit just as it is plucked from the tree, the greater will be the blessing."

"It would be well for us to do less cooking and to eat more fruit in its natural state. Eat freely of fresh grapes, apples, peaches, pears, berries and all other kinds of fruit that can be obtained."

Fruits supply sugar, acids, mineral matter and bulk. The mineral elements of fruits are more readily assimilated than those of flesh meat and vegetables. Acid fruits aid in the digestion of nuts and other nitrogenous foods. Acid, juicy fruits keep the system clean and free from germs. They render lime and soda salts soluble, enabling the system to throw them off. They *allay* instead of *creating* thirst. Alcohol and tobacco cannot stay long with the individual who uses no flesh foods and partakes freely of ripe juicy fruits. Use more fruit and fewer vegetables if you would not experience thirst.

Cane sugar is not digested in the stomach but causes fermentation by hindering the digestion of other foods. The sugar of fruits (grape and fruit sugar, so-called), and that of honey are all ready for assimilation, so require less labor on the part of the body and may be used more rapidly for the repair of muscular fatigue.

The laxative effect of fruit is very important. Very ripe bananas taken when the stomach is empty often produce immediate effect. Pineapples after nitrogenous foods, ripe olives, peaches, pears and nearly all fruits are helpful.

It is better to use the juice and pulp only, of seedy fruits like blackberries and black raspberries. With many people the seeds produce hives.

The matter of bulk in the diet is an important one. The whole digestive tract suffers if there is not a fairly good bulk of food to be handled by it, yet serious results follow when a large quantity of concentrated food is consumed; consequently, fruits and green vegetables being composed largely of water supply just what is needed.

Fruit must be thoroughly ripened, sound and well matured. Many unripe fruits contain raw starch which causes trouble when they are eaten.

The largest fruit of its kind is usually the cheapest. It is poor economy to spend money and (if the fruit requires paring) time, for seeds, skins, and cores. Besides, as a rule the larger fruit is more perfectly matured, so more wholesome as well as of a finer flavor.

Do not use the skins of fruits much. They are composed largely of woody fibre and are intended only for a covering to the fruit. In the days of stomach washes, the skins of fruits were noticeably abundant in the "unswallowed" food.

For the best effect, fruits should be used without sugar. When one has accustomed himself to the use of grape fruit and oranges without sugar, the addition of it will make them positively disagreeable to his taste, besides causing rebellion in the stomach.

Since acids hinder the digestion of starch, it is better to take acid fruits at the close of a meal including starchy foods, and we should especially avoid taking starches and acids into the mouth at the same time, before the starch has been acted upon by the saliva.

There is great opportunity for the display of artistic skill in serving fresh fruits, and nothing so well repays a little effort as the combination of leaves, ferns and vines with fruits. One beautiful dish that I remember was of plums, grapes and peaches with autumn leaves; another, with rich branches of foliage plants and a variety of fruits. Grape leaves combine beautifully with fruits.

One person with whom I am acquainted can use no starchy foods. The many attempts which she has made to use them invariably result in her becoming extremely weak, and helpless with rheumatism; but she thrives on a diet composed almost exclusively of acid fruits and nuts. She writes —"On my fruit and nut diet I seldom feel thirst, but after eating even starchless vegetables I suffer exceedingly from it. I find also that I do not require so much sleep as when living on another diet." Her chief fruits are sour apples, grape fruit, oranges and mealy-ripe bananas with a few raisins, dates and figs occasionally for dessert. She is at her best when currants are ripe; and takes them every day as long as they can be obtained.

APPLES

The apple, of which there are said to be over 2000 varieties, has no equal as an "all-round" fruit; but it is at its best just pared and eaten raw. It requires thorough mastication both for digestion and enjoyment.

When you are not feeling quite at par, cut an apple in two from stem to blossom end and with a round pointed knife scrape it into a fine pulp from either side. It is most refreshing and easily digested so. Children and people whose teeth are defective can take it best that way.

The apple is the choicest salad fruit.

BANANAS

The fact that the banana is a serious cause of indigestion when just turned yellow is quite generally understood, and fruit eaters now buy them and keep them until they become not just soft, but *mellow ripe*, which will be after the skins are dark or covered with dark spots. As long as they have a "pasty" feeling in the mouth they are unfit for food because the starch is not yet changed to sugar.

Do not try to hurry the ripening process as bananas are better when ripened slowly. Keep them in the dark, in a not too cold place and give them plenty of time. Large, plump bananas are far superior to small slender ones in wholesomeness and flavor, besides being cheaper.

There is no other way of using bananas to compare with eating them "out of hand" with the skin and fibres removed; but they may be served with sugar and lemon juice for luncheon or with whipped cream for dessert.

Almond cream is very harmonious with bananas. Peeled bananas with a little almond butter accompanying each mouthful make a complete and delightful luncheon. Brazil nut butter and cream are also excellent with bananas.

BLACKBERRIES

Wild blackberries are sweeter and finer flavored than cultivated ones and eaten in small quantities from the bush are very enjoyable, but they should not be taken in large quantities with their seeds. They may be served with nut, or whipped dairy cream. With a thin syrup of sugar and water they are delicious.

CANTALOUPE

Wash, drain, chill, cut in halves and remove the seeds with a round-pointed spoon (not a sharp pointed knife) or with the fingers. Do not put ice inside as it destroys the flavor. Serve on mat of grape leaves.

CURRANTS

Wash, drain, serve on the stems plain or around a mold of sugar (made by pressing not too dry powdered or granulated sugar into a small glass, and unmolding in the center of the plate), or a spoonful of sugar, on a dainty dish. Nice, very ripe currants are especially refreshing and reviving.

Frosted Currants

Pick fine even bunches of currants and dip them, one at a time, into a mixture of frothed white of egg and a very little cold water. Drain them until nearly dry and roll in powdered sugar. Repeat the dip in the sugar once or twice and lay them on white paper to dry. Use as a garnish.

DATES AND NUTS

Serve dates piled on a dessert plate with halves of nuts around, or on individual dishes with a spoonful of any desired nut butter or meal in the center of the dish.

DATES AND CREAM

Slice dates and cover with nut or dairy cream. Dairy cream may be whipped and piled in center of dish with fruit around.

DATES OR FIGS AND MILK

One writer on health subjects recommends dates and milk or figs and milk as an improvement upon bread and milk. They make an excellent combination and a satisfying meal.

Nut milk or nut cream are ideal for sweet fruits.

FIGS

Serve figs with nuts and with cream, the same as dates. For Stuffed Dates and Figs, see Confections.

GOOSEBERRIES

Nice large ripe gooseberries are most enjoyable right from the bushes.

GRAPES

There is perhaps no fruit more highly recommended than the grape. One says: "It is safe to say that the juice of no other fruit or vegetable so strikingly resembles blood in its composition as the unfermented juice of grapes."

Another: "Grapes eaten exclusively for several days bring about wonderful results in the system. From one to two pounds should be consumed daily at first, gradually increasing to eight or ten pounds."

The "grape cures" in France and Germany are too well known to require mention. There is said to be "a life giving principle in grapes which builds tissue and stimulates the sympathetic nervous system."

These quotations apply particularly to fresh grapes. Cooked grapes and juice do not agree with every one.

TO PACK GRAPES

Take the late grapes, pick them carefully, spread them in a cool place in layers on shelves, let them remain two weeks, then pack in barrels with dry hard-wood sawdust. Bran will answer very well. Packed in this manner the fruit will keep good through the winter it is said. After packing, grapes should be kept in a cool, dry place.

GRAPE FRUIT

Cut in halves crosswise, remove seeds with sharp pointed knife, and separate the pulp from the bitter membrane between the sections. Serve one half to each person in peel or small glass, or serve halves after removing seeds without separating pulp. The fruit should not be cut long before serving as the juice and pulp absorb the bitter of the cut membrane. Taken at the close of the meal, grape fruit is an aid to digestion. The effect will be better without sugar. As a dessert, it is sometimes served with a tablespoonful of thick maple syrup in the center.

GRAPE FRUIT WITH MALAGA GRAPES

Prepare grape fruit as for salad, combine with halved, seeded Malaga grapes and sugar; refill cups which have been wiped dry after standing in ice water.

Garnish with candied cherries or blanched almonds.

GRAPE FRUIT AMBROSIA

Mix grape fruit pulp with orange pulp, grated cocoanut and sugar. Serve, sprinkled with cocoanut, in its own cups or in glasses.

OLIVES

"When properly prepared, olives like nuts supply the place of butter and flesh meats. Oil as eaten in the olive is far preferable to animal oil or fat. It serves as a laxative. Its use will be found beneficial to consumptives and it is healing to an inflamed, irritated stomach."

The olive contains more protein than any of the other common fruits, and with the exception of the alligator pear is the only one containing any appreciable amount of oil. Until within a few years we have been eating this valuable fruit in its unripe state, but now we get it, both imported and home grown, ripe. There is just as much difference between a ripe and green olive as between a ripe and green apple.

The ripe olive is black or dark brown in color (according to where it was grown) and has its full quota of oil. After one has eaten ripe olives for a time, the green ones will have a harsh, rank taste to him. It is also much easier to acquire a taste for the ripe olive. The large, luscious ones with meat as thick as that of a good sized plum are truly delightful.

Those hurried on to the eastern market from California before the holidays are not thoroughly ripened, but there are some growers who hold them until properly matured before gathering. Olives are better just soaked a little and eaten in that state than to be used in cooked dishes; but when used in soups or sauces, add without cooking just before serving.

Ripe olives are a valuable substitute for butter with bread, giving an emulsified oil instead of a free fat, with no germs of tuberculosis or other diseases.

The dried olives sold by Italian grocers require a long soaking and several changes of water. They, too, become stronger flavored by cooking. They are considerably cheaper than the bottled ones but much less delicate in flavor.

ORANGES

"The one thing that quickest revives a human being is orange juice."—*Dr. Paul Edwards.*

"The orange is a fruit that is distinctly health-giving. Orange juice aids greatly in reducing the amount of putrefaction in the intestines of nearly all persons who are submitted to clinical laboratory tests."—*H. Irving Hancock, in "Good Housekeeping."*

The white separating membrane of the orange is rather indigestible, so in many cases it is better to use the juice or pulp only.

I am going to tell you how to "drink" oranges. First, cut the orange in halves from end to end, then cut each half in three or four pieces; place each one of these oblong cups to the lips and extract the juice, rejecting the seeds and leaving all the membrane. This method is most refreshing, if not elegant. Eaten with a spoon from the halves cut across is, next to this, most satisfying, but takes more time.

In Jamaica they peel off the outer yellow skin and cut the orange across into two unequal portions. They extract the juice and pulp from the larger stem section first, and reserve the smaller, sweeter section for the last.

Again, they peel the yellow part of the rind off about one-fourth of the way down, run the knife into the peeled end and cut away a conical portion of the pulp, thus opening all of the sections of the orange. They then suck out the juice, without any burned lips as the result.

One nice way to prepare the pulp is to peel the fruit as you would an apple, cutting deep enough to remove all the white portion of the covering; then to cut all around each section of pulp, just inside the separating membrane, when you can remove the pure pulp. Serve in glass sauce-dish, or in cups,—orange, glass or china.

Another dainty and satisfactory way of preparing an orange is to "cut two circles through the skin around the fruit about ½ in. apart and half way between the two ends. Remove all the rind except the half-inch band. Just over one of the natural separations between the sections of the orange, cut the band with a sharp knife. All the divisions may then be carefully separated one from another, while all remain attached to the girdle of yellow rind. Oranges may be laid in layers on a fruit plate, outstretched upon the narrow piece of peeling, or they may, after the several divisions have been carefully made, be closed together again. A ribbon tied around the orange over the rind girdle will preserve the spherical form and be very pretty and ornamental. It is but the act of a moment to untie this ribbon, when the sections will all lie before one in perfect readiness to be eaten."—*Clipping.*

PEACHES

Ripe mellow peaches are incomparable both for health and palatability. They are equally good both for grown people and children, though one writer says "the ripe mellow peach is really the child's fruit."

A friend fold me that an old Indian came to the house when her little brother was lying at the point of death, and said, "peach juice will keep him alive." The mother, anxious to leave nothing untried, began giving him the juice of stewed peaches, from which time he began to retain his food (the mother's milk) and to improve in every way. When he came to be weaned, peach juice and gradually the soft halves of peaches were his sole diet for eight months; then other foods were introduced sparingly, but all his life peaches have formed a large part of his diet and he is an unusually well man.

Wash and carefully rub peaches in cold water, and rub them well with a soft cloth in wiping to remove the down, which is irritating.

Peaches should ripen on the trees; the shipped ones are often suitable for cooking only as they are gathered before they are ripe. Some varieties are sour and disagreeable, while others are sweet and luscious.

Few people know how exceedingly delightful rich juicy white peaches are.

PEACHES AND CREAM

Pare peaches just as short a time before they are to be served as possible. Cut in halves, quarters or thick slices. Do not sweeten but pass sugar and unwhipped cream with them. Almond or cocoanut cream are especially suitable for peaches.

PEACH SNOW

Add sweetened cream to stiffly-beaten whites of eggs ($\frac{1}{3}$ cup to each white) and pour over peaches just before serving. All must be cold.

Peaches combine nicely with bananas and with red raspberries. The juice of the berries may be served over the peaches instead of cream.

PINEAPPLES

The pineapple is another of the universal favorites and deservedly. Its delightful flavor is unequaled and the fresh juice contains bromelin, a remarkably active principle which aids digestion both in the stomach and in the intestinal tract. A slice or two of pineapple taken at the close of a meal gives a marked laxative effect. The use of pineapple in diphtheria is well known. I knew a very successful physician in one of our large cities who always had quantities of pineapple canned each year for use in diphtheria cases. The digestive ferment is not quite so active in the cooked fruit as in the uncooked.

SHREDDED PINEAPPLE

Use only choice large well ripened sound pineapples. Wash and drain; give the crown a twist with the hand, when it will come out easily if the fruit is ripe. Set the pineapple on a board and with a large sharp knife pare it by cutting slices down from the top all around, cut thick enough to remove all the woody covering (the fruit in connection with that has very little flavor), leaving only the deepest eyes.

After removing the eyes, take the pineapple in the left hand with the base up and shred it by picking up small pieces all around with the tines of a silver fork. It will come off easily from that end, leaving the core, which should be wrung to obtain all the juice.

Let the fruit stand in layers with sugar, ¼ to ½ cup, (or ¼ to ⅓ cup sugar, ½ to 1 tablespn. lemon juice and ¾ cup water) to each pint, for some time before serving, or, serve plain and pass sugar with it. Pineapple and strawberries or raspberries or oranges with lemon juice and sugar are nice alone, or with cake, for dessert.

PINEAPPLE AND GRAPE FRUIT

Equal quantities of prepared pineapple and grape fruit with sugar and the juice of either poured over.

Peach, orange and pineapple is another nice combination.

PINEAPPLE AND WHIPPED CREAM

Drain finely-shredded pineapple and beat with whipped cream, as much as can be used and keep the combination stiff. Serve cold in glasses.

PINEAPPLE AND STRAWBERRY AMBROSIA

Equal quantities ripe strawberries, shredded pineapple and cream. Whip cream, place layer of pineapple in dish, sprinkle with sugar, cover with cream, then make a layer of strawberries, sugar and cream. Continue. Have cream on top. Serve cold with sponge cake or cocoanut crisps.

PINEAPPLE AND ORANGE AMBROSIA

Drained shredded pineapple, orange pulp and juice, grated cocoanut and sugar, in layers.

RAISINS

Raisins are nutritious and valuable foods, containing sometimes as high as 61 per cent. of grape sugar and a considerable proportion of albuminoids. They are suitably combined with all kinds of bread and nuts. One thing that makes them so satisfying is that they require thorough mastication.

RASPBERRIES—RED

When necessary to wash, have cold water in a deep pan and turn the berries in, not more than a quart at a time. (Do not pour the water over the berries as that bruises them.) Rinse up and down in the water with the hands and remove quickly to a colander. Drain, pile in dish and serve at once. Lemon or currant juice poured over makes a harmonious combination. ⅓ or ½ very ripe currants may be mixed with the berries. Serve Brazil nuts or blanched almonds with these combinations.

RASPBERRIES—BLACK

Black raspberries have a peculiar spicy flavor not found in any other fruit and when plump and thoroughly ripened may be used in moderate quantities in their natural state.

STRAWBERRIES

The perfect way to serve strawberries is the French—with the hulls on, without washing. Pass sugar with them, or pile the berries around a mold of sugar on individual plates, or, set a dainty cup or glass containing sugar in the center of the plate and pile the berries around. But if the berries are very sandy, wash the same as red raspberries. Wash berries always before hulling unless obliged to let stand after hulling, then do not wash until just ready to serve. The little strawberry hullers snip the hulls out so quickly and so perfectly without staining the fingers that they seem among the indispensables of housekeeping.

ORANGE STRAWBERRIES

Put sliced berries into glasses and pour sweetened orange juice over to more than cover. Let stand in a cool place 3 or 4 hrs. to improve the color. They may be served with an uncooked meringue garnished with halves or quarters of berries or a slice of orange.

WATERMELON

The flavor of watermelon is better if cooled in water instead of on ice. To serve cut the melon in halves across and cut off pieces from the ends so that they will stand. Serve the pulp by spoonfuls, scooped out with a tablespoon. If convenient take the pieces out before sending to the table, remove the seeds and return the pieces to the shell, then keep in a cool place until serving time.

The watermelon furnishes an abundance of pure distilled water. Watermelons that are not very sweet maybe served with almond cream and sugar.

WHORTLEBERRIES

The most desirable of this family is the large purple soft pulpy sweet juicy berry growing in the swamps, and called in some parts of the country "blueberry." It is delightful with nut or dairy cream or with sugar or in bread and milk. Its juice being so sweet it is one of the most suitable berries for sauce with cereals. In cakes puddings or pies it is equally enjoyable.

The so-called "huckleberry," though more seedy, has a nice flavor when cooked.

FRUITS—COOKED

APPLE SAUCE

Select nice tart apples; wash, drain, cut out the blossom end of each so that the little black particles will not get on to the fruit. Pare as thin as possible. When all are pared, cut into quarters, and core by cutting from both stem and blossom end downward to the center, just below the core. After coring, throw enough quarters into the kettle (granite, porcelain or aluminum) to about cover the bottom, and turn the quarters core side down. Then arrange another layer in the same way and continue until all are in. Pour boiling water over to half cover the apples (more or less according to the juiciness of the apples), cover kettle and set over hot fire. Cook without removing cover until apples are perfectly tender; remove from fire at once, stir in a little sugar if desired and a trifle of salt. This method gives a nice white well cooked sauce with a fresh apple taste. Placing the apples as directed causes them to cook tender quickly and evenly. The salt improves the flavor unless too much is used.

STRAINED APPLE SAUCE

When apples are small or knotty, cook without paring, rub through colander and add a little sugar.

BAKED APPLE SAUCE

Place quartered apples in pudding dish as for apple sauce. Sprinkle delicately with sugar between the layers and over the top. Pour water in at the side of the dish so as to leave the sugar on the top. Cover and bake for several hours until the apples assume a rich red color.

BAKED QUARTERS OF APPLES

Wash, quarter and core but do not pare apples; lay cut side down in pudding dish, pour very little if any water over, cover close, bake until tender. Remove cover and dry out well. Eat from the fingers, rejecting the skins, or scrape the pulp from the skin with a teaspoon. The skin imparts such richness and flavor to the pulp that it seems to have been sweetened with sugar.

BAKED APPLES

To the natural taste, the apple is best just washed, put into a baking pan with little if any water (depending upon the juiciness of the apple), covered at first and baked until tender and dry. Some prefer to have the apples cored with ½–1 teaspn. of sugar (brown sugar sometimes) placed in the core space.

LEMON APPLES, ORANGE APPLES, AND OTHERS

Core and pare nice large perfect apples. Place in the core space sugar with a little grated lemon or orange rind. Sprinkle outside of apples with sugar and turn a little lemon juice over for "Lemon Apples" or "Orange Apples." Bake until just tender, with or without a little water.

Use citron, cocoanut, raisins or nuts with sugar for other varieties. Fill core space with jelly for "Jelly Apples." Serve plain or with nut cream or whipped dairy cream, or with cocoanut or custard sauce or with wafers or nuts for dessert, at a meal without vegetables, especially starchy vegetables.

Lemon and jelly apples make suitable accompaniments to meat dishes.

BAKED SWEET APPLES

Bake whole with plenty of water at first (covered part of the time) until perfectly tender and all the water is evaporated. Serve for dessert, or for breakfast or supper with nuts, or with nut or dairy cream, or in bread and milk, than which nothing is more delicious.

"MOTHER" CRANSON'S STEWED SWEET APPLES

Put whole apples into preserving kettle, cover with thin syrup of sugar and water and cook until tender (carefully changing the apples from top to bottom once or twice) and the syrup just a little thick. Place the apples on plates and turn the syrup over.

STEWED BANANAS

Slice bananas, stew with a little sugar water and a trifle of ground or crushed anise seed tied in a piece of cheese cloth.

Prunes may be flavored the same.

BANANAS IN BUTTER

Simmer bananas in butter in an aluminum or agate frying pan covered, on the top of the stove where it is not too hot. They will not be browned but simply stewed.

BANANAS AND RAISINS

Cook raisins in a broad flat pan in water for an hour. Slice bananas over, cover and cook 10 m.

BAKED BANANAS

The simplest way to bake bananas is in the skins. It takes just 20 m. in a moderate oven. To eat, strip a piece of skin about an inch wide from the top side and partake of the baked fruit from the remaining skin in teaspoonfuls.

Bananas may be baked whole with a little water after peeling, and served with orange or cream sauce.

A little melted butter may be poured over bananas before baking or they may be rolled in lemon juice and sugar and baked. For a richer dish, turn mixed melted butter, sugar and lemon juice over bananas in lengthwise halves in agate pan. Bake 15–20 m. in slow oven. Serve with meat dishes sometimes.

BAKED CRUMBED BANANAS

Roll peeled bananas in fine granella, cracker or zwieback crumbs mixed with sugar. Bake in moderate oven till just tender. Serve at once.

BANANAS BAKED WITH TOMATOES

Put a thin layer of stewed or sliced tomatoes in the bottom of a baking pan. Cover with bananas sliced crosswise. Bake.

CRANBERRIES

Cranberries are said to "promote digestion and purify the blood." There is no question but they are a desirable fruit and should be used freely in their season.

Stewed Cranberries

1 qt. berries,

¾ cup sugar,

1–1½ cup water.

Pour boiling water over cranberries, let stand 2 m., or until cold; drain, add sugar and water, cook covered, until boiling all through. Rub through colander if the skins are objectionable. 2–3 tablespns. of lemon juice and more sugar may be added.

Baked Cranberries.

Make syrup of 1 pt. of water and 1½ cup of sugar; boil, cool. Pour over 1 qt. of cranberries in baking dish. Bake until clear.

Cranberries With Raisins

1 qt. berries

¾–1 cup seeded raisins

1 cup sugar

1 pint water

Stew raisins in water until nearly tender; pour boiling water over cranberries and drain; cook all together until berries are done.

A larger proportion of raisins and less sugar may be used.

BAKED PEACHES

Whole, pared, cling-stone peaches; sugar, butter and lemon juice. Bake 40 m. May be served with meat dishes, or as dessert.

BAKED QUINCES—Delicious

Wash, pare, halve, core. (Save skins and cores for jelly). Cover with a large quantity of thin sugar and water syrup. Bake covered, basting often and turning occasionally until tender and the syrup rich. Uncover at the last for a short time.

PLAIN BAKED QUINCES

Pare and core quinces, bake with water only, basting. Serve with hard or creamy sauce or with nut cream and sugar.

RHUBARB

Rhubarb is not a fruit but the stalk of the plant and as its acid is oxalic, it is a somewhat questionable article of diet. At all events it should not be used freely.

Stewed Rhubarb

1 qt. rhubarb
½ cup sugar

Wash rhubarb, do not peel, cut into ¾ in. pieces; cook with sugar, on the back of the stove until juicy; then stew till tender.

Stewed Rhubarb, No. 2

1 qt. rhubarb
scant ⅔ cup sugar
1 tablespn. lemon juice
¼ cup water

Cook all together.

Baked Rhubarb

Put rhubarb in baking dish with sugar and lemon juice as for stewing, with or without a little water. Cover and bake until tender.

It is said that if young cherry leaves are scalded and the juice added to cooked rhubarb, it will impart the flavor of cherries to the rhubarb.

STEWED DRIED FRUITS

The flavors of dried fruits are more natural and delicate with prolonged soaking and short (if any) cooking. Choice dried apples and apricots are especially enjoyable soaked over night or longer without any cooking. The juice from them makes an exceedingly refreshing drink.

Pour boiling water over fruit that requires washing to more perfectly loosen the dirt, then quickly add cold water. Wash thoroughly, cover with warm water and let stand for from 12 to 48 hrs. When perfectly swollen and soft, add sugar, if it is to be used, bring to the boiling point quickly and remove from the fire. These directions if followed will cause apples, apricots and peaches to seem almost like fresh stewed fruit.

A few fresh grapes stewed with peaches give them a nice flavor.

Raisins also (previously cooked) are nice with dried peaches.

The most delightful combination with dried apples is ⅓ prunelles. Raisins are also nice with apples.

Stewed Dried Apricots

½ lb. apricots
3½ cups water

½ cup sugar

Follow general directions.

PRUNES—SWEET CALIFORNIA

These require no sugar but will bear a little longer cooking than peaches and apricots.

¾ prunes and ¼ apricots make a nice combination, also raisins or figs and prunes.

Prune Marmalade

Cook prunes with a small amount of water and rub through colander. This removes the skins or breaks them up so that many can take them who otherwise could not. Served with almonds, beaten white of egg or almond or whipped cream, the marmalade makes a nice dessert.

Steamed Prunes—par excellence

Soak large prunes in a very little water, stirring occasionally so that all will be moistened. Steam ¾ of an hour. Cover as soon as removed from the steamer. Serve warm for breakfast. They may be steamed an hour without soaking.

Stewed Figs

Wash, soak, cook until tender, reduce liquor to syrup and pour over fruit. Serve with wafers or nuts or with whipped cream flavored with vanilla or almond.

Steamed Figs—best of all

Wash figs and steam 25–35 m. according to dryness. Long steaming gives them a strong flavor. Cover, and serve warm. The figs may be soaked the same as prunes before steaming.

Fruit Butter

Stew together 1½ lb. prunes and 1 lb. of dried apricots, no sugar. Rub through colander and cook to the consistency of butter.

TO CAN FRUITS

Suggestions

The best quality of aluminum is the ideal material for the preserving kettle; but granite, porcelain or earthenware may be used.

Thorough sterilization of the jars or cans is one of the most important parts of fruit canning. I always wash and sterilize mine when I empty them.

After washing the covers of Mason jars, bake them in a moderate oven for 2 or 3 hours; scrape them on the inside if necessary but do not wet them, and screw them on to the jars, which should have been well washed, scalded, wiped with a clean towel and thoroughly dried by standing right side up in a warm place.

The rubbers should be put on when the covers are, so that the jars will be all ready for use.

When old rubbers are in good condition they are just as good as new ones. Sometimes two thin ones may be used together.

There is a certain black rubber that should not be used with delicate flavored fruits as it injures their flavor. It does not improve the flavor of any fruit.

New rubbers should be washed and rubbed well in soapsuds and rinsed before using.

Keep the jars in a dry place and when you come to use them turn them over once in a pan of boiling water, scalding the covers the same.

Do not waste time, strength, jars or sugar on imperfect, decayed or unripe fruit. The probabilities are that it will not keep; and if it does the appearance and flavor will be inferior.

Put the fruit into the jars *boiling hot* and seal immediately. Do not try to remove the froth or air bubbles (pure air will do no harm in cans, and it will be pure when the fruit is at boiling heat all around it and will remain so if the can is well sealed), because while you are trying to let the air out the fruit is cooling on top and the germs from the outside air are settling upon it.

If the fruit gets below the boiling point while filling the jars, return it to the fire and reheat it. *Fill the jars to overflowing.* Fasten the covers on perfectly tight, press the edges down all around into the rubber of Mason jars, if inclined to leak. Do not tighten the covers after the fruit is cold.

With Lightning jars it is sometimes necessary to slip little splinters of wood (bits of berry boxes) under the wires to make the covers tight enough.

When the covers are perfectly adjusted, invert the jars and leave them until cool. This not only shows whether any are leaking or not but fills any spaces there may be.

Keep canned fruit in a dark place. The light will cause it to lose its flavor as well as color. Wrap jars in paper if necessary.

The simplest way to fill jars is to set them in a row on a towel wrung out of cold water and folded so that it is thick. The jars must be cold also. Or, the towel may be wrung out of hot water and the jars rinsed in hot water before filling. In either case have the covers warm.

Bear in mind that "sugar, when largely used, is more injurious than meat."

Some fruits, rich fine-flavored pears and peaches, whortleberries and others are excellent canned without sugar. They taste more like fresh fruit.

I always can whortleberries without water, so as to have them for pies. For sauce, water may be added after they are opened.

Gooseberries canned without water or sugar make delightful, fresh tasting pies in winter.

Never fail to secure black currants if possible for pies.

Always label fruit before putting it away, giving the year in which it was put up.

Canned fruits and vegetables should be opened two hours or more before serving, to give the fresh taste which comes with the restoration of oxygen.

There is much work at the best connected with fruit canning, so I have tried to simplify it as much as possible. The methods given here are those which I have used for years with good results.

TO CAN SOLID BERRIES

Cherries, whortleberries, red and black currants and all berries that do not crush easily may be put into the kettle in layers with sugar (never more than ½ pt. of sugar to 2 qts. of fresh fruit and usually less), brought to the boiling point slowly and put into jars with very little trouble. The following is an average proportion of sugar and water to use with this class of berries:

Blackberries—2 qts. berries. ½–¾ cup sugar, 2 cups water.

Blk. Raspberries—2 qts. berries, ½–¾ cup sugar, 2 cups water.

Gooseberries, green—2 qts. berries, 1–1½ cup sugar, 4 cups water.

Gooseberries, ripe—2 qts. berries, 1–1½ cup sugar, 1–1½ cup water.

Whortleberries,—2 qts. berries, ½ cup sugar (if any), 1 tablespn. water.

Rhubarb—1 qt. rhubarb in ¾ in. lengths, ½ cup sugar, no water.

TO CAN PEACHES AND FRUITS OF THAT CLASS

Peaches

Wash peaches, rubbing well, drain, pare as thin as possible and drop into cold water to keep them from turning dark. If the peaches are very ripe, put a few at a time into a wire basket and plunge into boiling water. Hold them there a moment, then quickly turn them into cold water; after which the skins will slip off easily.

This is a quicker method and does not waste the peaches, but I have thought they were more apt to turn dark.

For each rounded quart of peaches, make a syrup of ⅓–½ cup of sugar and 1–1½ cup of water, the water in which the peaches were standing. Bring the syrup to the boiling point, drop the peaches in (if in halves the cut side down), boil until thoroughly heated through, or until tender; drop the peaches into the jars, pour boiling syrup over, seal, following "Suggestions" carefully.

Pears

1 rounded qt. (8 or 9) pears in halves
⅓–½ cup sugar
1 tablespn. lemon juice

1–1½ cup water

Finish the same as peaches.

The lemon juice gives character to the pears.

I once had some pears that were so flavorless it seemed hardly worth while to can them, but I tied ground anise seed in small pieces of cheese cloth and cooked with them, besides adding lemon juice, and they were excellent. Small pears and those with thin skins may be canned without paring. They are richer but the skins sometimes cause flatulence.

Do not can pears while they are hard.

Plums

1 qt. plums
¼–⅓ cup sugar
¼–½ cup water

It is a good plan to prick the plums on all sides with a fork before cooking.

Quinces and Sweet Apples

6 qts. quinces in eighths
6 qts. sweet apples in quarters
5 qts. water
4–6 cups sugar

Cook quinces in water until tender, remove with skimmer; cook apples in same water, remove apples, measure water, adding more if necessary; dissolve sugar in water, heat to boiling, add fruit, simmer a few minutes and put into jars.

Quinces are much improved by combining with sweet apples. When the apples are cooked with them, the quinces become more tender.

Quinces and citron and quinces and pears may also be combined.

Cranberries and Sweet Apples

1 qt. cranberries

1½ qt. sweet apples in quarters

⅔ qt. cold water

¾–1 cup sugar

Cook sugar, water and cranberries together, until the cranberries begin to crack; add the apples and cook all slowly until the apples are soft. Put into jars and seal.

To Can Strawberries

Also red raspberries and all delicate berries.

For each 2 qts. of hulled berries (just enough to fill one quart jar), use 1 cup of granulated sugar. Put a layer of berries into an earthen or granite ware dish, sprinkle with sugar, cover with another layer of berries and so on. (Strawberries are so juicy they will not bear any water). Let berries and sugar stand together in the ice box or cellar for several hours. They may be prepared late in the afternoon and put into the jars the first thing the next morning.

When ready to can the fruit, drain off the juice, heat it to boiling, turn the berries carefully into it and shake and turn the dish once in a while to keep the fruit heating evenly. When just boiling all through, dip carefully into cans with a handled cup. Put the covers on quickly, no matter how many bubbles of air there are nor how much froth there is in the jars, and screw down tight with a can opener. After pressing the edge of the covers down if necessary, lay the jars on the side (instead of inverting, for strawberries) and turn over occasionally while cooling.

When perfectly cold, set jars upright and you will find the berries evenly distributed through the jars and they will never rise to the top.

Allowing the berries to stand in sugar and afterwards putting them into boiling syrup hardens them so that they keep their shape. It is better to heat just enough at once to fill each jar. You can have several dishes (milk crocks, granite, porcelain and aluminum kettles) on the stove at once at different stages of heating so that you can fill one jar after another.

This was my auntie's method and I have never seen it excelled.

Pineapple

¼–⅓ cup sugar

½–1 tablespn. lemon juice
¾ cup water
1 pt. pineapple

Prepare pineapple as for fresh pineapple, put into stone jars or earthen vessels with layers of sugar; stand in ice box a few hours (not long enough to ferment), drain off the juice, add lemon juice and water, heat to boiling, add fruit. Let all just boil up, fill jars, seal as other fruits. The delicate flavor of pineapple is lost by long cooking.

Grated pineapple canned with ½ cup of sugar to the quart is suitable for ices and other uses.

Rhubarb—cooked

Put stewed rhubarb into jars as soon as it boils up well.

Rhubarb Without Cooking—for pies
A reliable method which gives the natural flavor.

Wash rhubarb and cut into inch pieces without peeling, pour boiling water over, drain at once, cool, pack in cans and fill with boiled, strained, ice-cold water. Seal cans, invert in cold place and cover from the light. Set upright after a few hours. To use, drain, let stand in fresh cold water ½ hour and drain again.

Cranberries may be canned in the same way.

Watermelon Rind or Citron

Pare off the thin green rind, cut into pieces 1 in. square, or into strips, stand in cold water for two or three hours, changing the water occasionally; drain thoroughly, make syrup of 1 pt. water to 1 or 1½ pt. sugar, according to the richness desired. (3 or 4 tablespns. of lemon juice may be used with the larger quantity of sugar). When syrup is boiling, add rind, simmer until pieces can be pierced easily with a broom straw, or until they are clear, put into jars and seal.

One part raisins to five or six of the rind gives a nice flavor. Or, orange flowers, rose leaves or rose water may be used, but the fruit is nice without any flavoring.

Green melons which did not have time to ripen before the frost, are excellent prepared in this way.

The rind may be steamed before putting it into the syrup, and less water used for the syrup.

Concord Grapes

2 qts. grapes
¾ cup sugar
½ cup water

Pulp the grapes, run skins through the food cutter and cook for 20 m. in the water. Boil pulp until tender and rub through colander to remove the seeds. Add pulp and sugar to skins, heat to boiling and put into jars. The juice may be strained from the pulp and used to cook the skins in.

Barberries

1 qt. berries
2 cups sugar
½–1 cup water

Very nice for garnishing fruit salads, desserts or cakes.

Tomatoes

Select only perfectly fresh, well ripened tomatoes, wash and drop into kettle of boiling water, remove with skimmer, drop into cold water, peel, leave whole or slice. Boil well and put into jars the same as other fruit. Long boiling frees the acid and takes away the fresh, delicate flavor. When tomatoes are very watery, drain off some of the liquid and can it separately for use in soups and broths.

Tomatoes for Soups and Sauces

Wash and slice tomatoes without peeling. Heat to boiling, rub through fine colander or sieve to remove skins and seeds. Reheat and put into jars.

Whole Tomatoes

Pack peeled or unpeeled tomatoes in wide-mouthed jars. Cook a few nice ripe tomatoes, strain and pour the liquid, cold, over tomatoes in jars, seal, set jars in cold water as in canning vegetables, bring slowly to boiling point and boil ½ hour. Remove from water, tighten covers and invert jars as usual.

FRUIT JUICES

Begin with the earliest fruits and can some of the juice of each kind through the summer until you come to grapes and apples in the autumn. When diluted with water, these juices are delightful beverages for sick or well. A little lemon juice gives character to the drink. Without diluting, they make nice flavorings for fruit salads, egg creams and pudding sauces. Blueberry, black raspberry and other sweet juices make excellent dressings for grains instead of milk or cream.

Grape Juice

Concords or some of the dark purple grapes are the richest and most satisfactory for juice. Pick the grapes from the stems, wash and drain, put into a preserving kettle without water, cover and put on back of stove on an asbestos pad or a ring so they will heat slowly. When the skins are broken and the juice is free, bring just to the boiling point, put into jelly bags and drain without squeezing. To each quart of juice add from ½ to 1 cup of sugar. Very ripe grapes will require no sugar. Heat to boiling and can the same as fruit.

Add more water to the pulp that is left in the jelly bag, reheat, strain, boil and put into large jars for a drink, or, rub the pulp through a colander, sweeten, heat and can for marmalade.

To Bottle Juices—Nearly fill bottles, standing on cloth wrung out of cold water, with boiling juice, through hot funnel. Press clean cork into bottle, cut off even with the top of the bottle and cover immediately with sealing wax made by melting together resin and oil. Use only enough oil to make the resin soft enough to spread over the cork and around the edges of the bottle. If too soft, the wax will run off.

Condensed Fruit Juices

Cook apple and other fruit juices rapidly until thick, then simmer slowly over the fire or in the oven until as thick as desired. Seal in jars or put into glasses or cups as jelly. Convenient for travelling, diluted.

APPLES

When apples are plentiful or likely to spoil, make into any of the apple sauces, put hot into jars and seal.

Baked Apples

Bake unpared apples, sweet or sour, in halves or quarters, leaving them rather juicy, put into jars and seal. On opening, put apples into oven in baking dish and dry out a little more.

Combinations of Fruits for Canning

Red or black raspberries with currant juice.
    Red or black raspberries with cherries.
    Plums with sweet apples.
    Currants or currant juice with pineapple.
    Orange, strawberry and pineapple juices with sugar, for strawberries and pineapple canned together, or for pineapple alone.
    Strawberries with pineapple.
    Pears and barberries. Cook barberries in water, rub through colander, add sugar, 1–1½ cup to the pint of pulp. Return to the fire and when hot, lay in halves or quarters of nice ripe pears. Cook until pears are tender. If the pears are not quite soft, steam, or cook in pulp without sugar first. Sweet apples may be used instead of pears.

JELLIES

Because of the large proportion of sugar required in jellies it is not best to use them freely.

Fruit for jelly should always be a little underripe and should not be picked just after a rain. Combine the juices of such fruits as do not jelly easily, or of the more expensive fruits, with apple juice which jellies the easiest of all. With strong flavored fruits, apple makes the jelly more agreeable. Jellies may be made in the winter of canned fruit juices and the juice from apple skins and cores. The addition of lemon juice to sweet fruits will convert them into jelly-making products. A few pieces of rose geranium leaves dropped into apple jelly just before putting it into glasses and removed in a minute, give the jelly a nice flavor.

Always boil the juice the required length of time before adding the sugar. It requires longer boiling on damp days.

Heat sugar in flat pan in oven before adding to jelly.

Thorough straining is necessary to make clear jelly. For the finest jelly, use first a double thickness of mosquito netting; then the same of cheese cloth, and lastly, one thickness of flannel.

Wet the cloth before putting the fruit in, to save the waste of juice. Hang in a warm place to drain.

It is said that if a little jelly dropped into cold water falls immediately to the bottom, the jelly is done; or, if it jellies on the spoon it is done.

Glasses for jelly may be set cold on a cold cloth, or warm on a warm cloth. Fill to the brim, as the jelly shrinks.

When the jelly is soft, set in the sun for a day or two, covered with panes of glass. When ready to set away, turn hot melted paraffine over the jelly. The heat destroys any germs which may have settled on the top. Cover with paper or with tin covers and set in a dark place. When using the jelly, wash and save the paraffine.

If jelly is to be moved or shipped, use a covering of ¼ inch of powdered sugar instead of the paraffine.

Or, cut rounds of toilet paper, two for each glass, large enough to overlap an inch; dip one at a time into a saucer of cold boiled milk, cover glass and press down, then put on the second piece quickly.

One thickness of Manila paper may be used instead of the toilet paper. When dry, a thick parchment-like cover will be formed and the jelly will keep well. Some housewives cover jelly while hot, thinking it keeps better.

To Make Jelly Tumblers

Soak a cord in turpentine, tie it tight around bottles and set fire to the cord.

Currant Jelly

Wash and drain currants. They are usually left on the stems but strain more easily if stemmed. Crush the berries, a few at a time and throw into the preserving kettle. Do not add any water. Set on back of range and heat slowly to nearly, not quite, boiling. Strain, measure juice, return to kettle and set over fire. At the same time put into a moderate oven in broad bottomed pans, sugar in the proportion of ¾–1 pt. to each pint of juice (¾ is sufficient). After juice begins to boil, boil 20 m., skimming as the scum rises. Add hot sugar, stir until sugar is dissolved, remove from fire and put at once into glasses.

⅓ white currants may be used with red.

A thinner jelly to be used with meats and over puddings underneath the meringue, may be made with ½ pt. of sugar to the pint of juice.

A little celery salt may be added when jelly is to be used with meats.

Currant and Raspberry Jelly

⅔ currant juice and ⅓ raspberry or ⅓ currant and ⅔ raspberry makes a delightful combination.

Black Currant Jelly

Prepare stemmed currants as for red currant jelly. Use ¼ to ½ cup of water to each quart of currants and ¾ pt. of sugar to a pint of juice. 10 m. boiling is sufficient.

½ or ⅔ apple juice will make a more delicate flavored jelly.

Jelly of Apple Parings and Cores

Measure skins and cores by pressing firmly into the measure. Add ⅓ (no more) as much water as of fruit—you will think it is not enough. Boil 20 m., stirring often. Strain. Measure juice, boil 20–30 m., according to juiciness of apples, skimming. Add ½ as much sugar, hot, as of juice, boil 5–10 m., or until foamy. Put at once into glasses.

If apple jelly is as thick as desired when it first cools, it will be too thick after standing a few days. If apples are very juicy, use only one-half as much water.

Apple Jelly

Wash apples and cut into quarters or eighths. Do not pare or core. Add ¼ as much water as of apples in the kettle. Cook, stirring occasionally until apples are tender, not too soft. Finish as in jelly of parings. It is difficult to give the exact time for cooking, as apples vary in jellying properties. Use less water if apples are very juicy. One quince to every 10 or 12 apples gives a nice flavor. A few green grapes combined with apples or crab apples make a nice jelly.

Crab and Baldwin apples may be combined.

Apple and Cranberry Jelly

Stew 1 qt. of apple parings with 1 cup of cranberries and a pint of water until tender. Strain. There should be about ¾ of a pint of juice. Boil 5 m.; add ¾ pt. sugar, boil 2–4 m. Or, use 1 doz. large tart apples to 1 qt. of berries, or equal parts apple and cranberry juice. Proceed as in other jellies.

Elder-berry and Apple Jelly

Cook elder-berries with ½ cup of water to each quart of berries. Strain and combine with apple juice in the proportion of ⅓ elder-berry juice to ⅔ apple juice. Use ¾–1 pt. of sugar to each pint of juice. Finish as for currant jelly. Elder-berries alone make a strong flavored jelly, but this combination is delightful.

Strawberries, raspberries, blackberries, cherries, wild cherries, pineapple, barberries, peaches, plums and some other fruits, all make better jelly by combining with apple juice in proportions according to flavor. Use no water with any of the fruits but the apple.

Currant juice may be combined with these fruits instead of apple juice.

Green Gooseberry Jelly

2 qts. berries, ¾ qt. water; stew, mash, strain; boil 20 m. for each quart of juice, add 1 qt. of hot sugar, boil 2–3 minutes.

Quince Jelly

Wash quinces, cut into quarters or eighths, remove part or all of the seeds, use ⅓–½ as much water as of fruit and ½ as much sugar as of juice. Cook and finish as apple jelly.

⅓–½ apple juice with quince is better.

Cranberry Jelly

Use one cup of water to each 4 qts. of cranberries; cook until the berries are tender, strain and use equal quantities of sugar and juice. Boil the juice 10–12 m., add the sugar hot, stir till it is dissolved and turn the jelly into glasses or a mold. The jelly may be molded in a shallow pan and when perfectly cold cut into cubes.

Jellied Cranberry Pulp

Rub stewed cranberries in the preceding recipe through the colander, boil 8 m., add sugar, stir carefully until dissolved, mold.

Jellied Cranberry Sauce

1 qt. berries, 1 pt. sugar, ½–1 cup water. Pour water over berries with sugar, in kettle, cover, cook 10 m. without stirring. Put into large or individual molds. Unmold at serving time.

Blueberry Jelly

If berries are very dry, add a little water, heat, strain; use ½–¾ as much sugar as of juice.

Blueberry Jelly No. 2

4 qts. berries, 1 cup water; cook and strain, add 2 tablespns. of lemon juice to each pint of juice. Cook 20 m., add ¾ as much sugar, hot, as of juice, boil up well, pour into glasses.

Grape Jelly

Wild grapes are preferable, but underripe Concords, Catawbas, and other varieties may be used.

Proceed as for currant jelly, using only ⅔ as much sugar as of juice. If necessary, boil 5 m. after sugar is added. Use no water with cultivated grapes, but with underripe wild grapes, ½ cup of water may be added to each quart of stemmed grapes.

Raspberry and Currant Jam

Take ¾ their weight of sugar to berries. Mash berries in kettle over fire, add 1 pt. currant juice to each 2 qts. of berries, cook until thickened, 40–45 m., stirring and skimming, add sugar hot, boil, put into glasses or seal in jars.

Strawberry Jam

Allow ¾ their weight of sugar to berries; cook in a little of the sugar, stirring, 20–30 m. Add remainder of sugar hot, cook 10–20 m., if necessary. Small berries may be used for jam.

Gooseberry Jam

Press the juice from 3 oranges and shave off the rind, being careful not to get any of the white part. Remove blossoms and stems from 5 lbs. gooseberries, seed 2 lbs. of raisins, and chop all together very fine. Add 3–4 lbs. sugar and the orange juice and cook slowly for an hour. Turn into jars or tumblers and when cold spread a layer of powdered sugar on top of glass and seal.

Mrs. Chandler's Rhubarb Jam

3 lbs. (3½ qts.) of rhubarb in inch lengths
1½ lb. (3 cups) sugar
½ lb. of figs or raisins, chopped
juice of 1 lemon
1 cup water

Let rhubarb and sugar stand together over night, add other ingredients and cook slowly for about 3 hours.

Rhubarb and Pineapple Jam

6 lbs. (7 qts.) rhubarb in inch lengths
1 large pineapple, grated
3 lbs. (3 pints) sugar

Cook rhubarb and sugar ½–¾ of an hour, add pineapple, boil up, put into jars, seal.

Melrose Apple Butter

7 lbs. pared, quartered and cored apples, 3 lbs. molasses sugar if obtainable, if not, dark brown sugar. Put apples and sugar in layers in a kettle, cover tight, let stand 12 hours or over night. Then let come just to boiling and simmer without stirring, or uncovering for 5–12 hours.

Apple juice made by boiling the skins of apples in ⅓ their bulk of water, as for jelly, with lemon juice to taste, is a valuable addition. Finely-ground coriander seed may be added. A little date or prune marmalade may also be used.

A delightful butter may be made by combining plums and apples.

Elder-berry and Apple Butter

To each 2 qts. of elder-berry juice prepared as for jelly take 2 lbs. brown sugar and ½ peck sour apples. Put juice and sugar on to boil and add the apples pared, quartered and cored; simmer slowly until thick. May be put into jelly glasses.

Equal quantities tomato and apple make a nice butter.

Grape Marmalade

Pulp the grapes and put the skins through the food cutter. Cook the pulp and rub through the colander to remove the seeds. Take ½–¾ as much sugar as there is of fruit, cook 20 m. The skins improve the flavor.

Lemon Peaches

1 cup lemon juice
1 cup water
1 cup brown sugar
peaches to fill 3 pint jars

Wash and rub the peaches well, drop into boiling syrup of lemon juice, sugar and water, cook until tender, put into jars and seal.

Ripe Cucumber Pickles

Pare and seed cucumbers and cut into eighths if large. Soak over night in lemon juice and water; in the morning drain, add to hot syrup and boil until soft; skim out of syrup and put into jars standing in hot water. Keep hot. Boil syrup 10–15 m., pour over fruit and seal; let stand three or four weeks before using.

Syrup—
    3 cups brown sugar
    3 cups lemon juice
    1 cup water
    ½–1 tablespn. salt

Flavor with celery salt or seed, ground coriander or anise seed, and raisins to taste. (Use anise seed sparingly). The cucumbers may be steamed tender, put into jars and the reduced syrup poured over.

Watermelon rind may be prepared the same.

To Dry Blueberries
For buns, puddings and cakes.

    1 qt. berries
    ⅓–½ cup sugar
    1 teaspn. water

Mix, heat in preserving kettle until juice begins to exude. Spread on buttered plates, dry carefully, stirring often.

I prize this recipe highly, as all will, I am sure, after trying it. Cherries, peaches and pears are better with sugar sprinkled over them before drying.

Dried fruits make a pleasant change from canned ones, besides not requiring jars. Home-dried fruit far excels factory products.

TO CAN VEGETABLES

While vegetables require a little more care than fruit in canning, if they receive that care one will be rewarded with nice fresh canned vegetables, free from harmful preservatives, all through the winter.

In the first place, vegetables must be fresh, especially corn and peas. Corn gathered early in the morning ought to be in the cans and on the fire before noon, and peas the same day.

If one is alone with all the housework to do, it is better to put up a few jars at a time.

Always use new rubbers on jars in canning vegetables.

"Blanching", in this connection, means a short boiling in a weak brine (¼ cup of salt to 3 qts. of water) and is used with vegetables to eliminate the acids which they contain.

Place the vegetables in a wire basket or a cloth bag and dip into the boiling brine, then into cold water.

Prepare nearly all vegetables as for the table, before blanching, (okra and corn are exceptions).

After blanching, pack as close as possible in jars. Fill jars to overflowing with water with or without salt, according to special directions; fasten covers on tight (do not be afraid the jars will burst), and set into a kettle or boiler with a board containing holes or with several thicknesses of cloth or with thin tin rings underneath. Surround jars ¾ their depth with water, cover the vessel close so that the steam will be retained, bring to the boiling point and boil rapidly and continuously the required length of time.

Use wrench for tightening covers of Mason jars during the cooking. If Lightning jars do not seem to be air-tight, thin bits of wood may be placed under the wires. With corn and peas, it is better to have the water deep enough to cover the jars, for boiling after tops are tightened.

Invert jars after removing from the water, cover to exclude light, cool.

Store in dark, rather cool place.

Use cold water to surround jars at first if contents are cold and warm water if contents are warm.

The length of time given is for cooking quart jars. ½–1 hour less will be required for pints and 1 hour more for 2 quarts.

Asparagus—Prepare asparagus as for the table; blanch tips 3 m., other parts 5 m., dip in cold water, pack in jars—the tips in one, the middle of the stalks in a second, and the inferior ends for soups, in a third.

Fill jars with cold water to which salt has been added in the proportion of 1 teaspn. to the quart.

Fasten covers and cook according to general directions for two hours, tighten covers and cook for one hour longer.

Asparagus in Full Lengths—Place stalks in jars, heads up, and pack as close as possible.

To Use—Open jar, add ½ teaspn. salt, set jar in cold or lukewarm water, heat to boiling, pour water off (save for soups), and draw stalks out carefully on to slices of prepared toast.

Shelled Beans—Follow directions for canning asparagus.

String Beans—Prepare as for the table or leave whole, blanch for 2 m., and follow directions for canning asparagus, using water without salt to fill the jars.

Greens—Narrow dock, milkweed, pigweed, purslane or spinach. Wash the greens thoroughly, drop into boiling salted water and leave just long enough to wilt. Remove from water with skimmer, pack into jars, cover with cold salted water and proceed as with other vegetables.

There are no vegetables that we enjoy more in winter than our "greens."

Okra—Wash young tender okra, cut off stems and tops, blanch 10 m., dip in cold water, cut in transverse slices or leave whole, and finish the same as asparagus.

Peas—Blanch fresh-gathered, mature, but not old peas, for 5 m. (old for 8 m.), dip in cold water, proceed as for canning asparagus, using sugar, 1 teaspn. to quart of water if peas are not sweet. Boil 3–4 hrs. in all; 1 hr. after tightening covers, with water covering jars if possible.

Corn—Prepare fresh-gathered corn as for drying. Pack at once (filling all spaces) in clean jars to within an inch of the top, cover to the depth of a half inch with slightly salted water, fasten covers on as tight as possible, cook 3 or 4 hours, screw covers down again, cover jars with boiling water and boil for 1 hour longer. Remove boiler from fire and let jars cool in the water.

Ears of corn may be boiled in clear water 5 m. and dropped in cold water before removing kernels.

Corn No. 2—Prepare as in preceding recipe and cook for 1 hr. after the water is boiling; tighten covers, invert and leave until the next day. Cook for 1 hr. the second day and again the third day, that is, 1 hr. each for three consecutive days.

Beets—Boil small dark red beets for 30 m., drop into cold water and rub the skins off. Place in jars, cover with cold water, fasten covers, boil 1 hr., tighten covers and boil for 1 hr. longer.

Mushrooms—Pour boiling salted water over mushrooms and allow them to stand in a warm place until withered; cool, drain, pack close in jars and cover with the water in which they were standing; seal and cook 1½ hr. Tighten covers and cook ½ hr. longer. Invert jars until cool.

TO DRY VEGETABLES

Corn—Boil corn 2–5 m., score down the center of each row of grains with a sharp knife. With a large sharp knife cut off the thinnest possible layer from each two rows, then with a dull case-knife scrape out the pulp from the hulls on the cob. Mix pulp with that which was cut off, spread on plates or granite pans and dry in a warm oven, stirring often. If the oven is too warm, the corn will turn dark. Corn may be dried in the sun if it is hot, but must be brought in before the dew begins to fall and spread out in the house. It is better to dry a little at a time in the oven and have it out of the way in a few hours. With proper care it can be done in an afternoon.

When dry, put at once into dry clean jars and seal, or into paper sacks tied tight so that no insects can get at it.

With care to keep it from souring, the corn may be dried without cooking.

Any dried corn has a richer flavor than canned corn, but words are inadequate to express how rich and fine flavored the yellow sweet corn is when dried.

Corn for drying should be nice and tender; a little younger, if anything, than for cooking green.

Directions for cooking dried corn are among the vegetables.

Shelled Beans—Lima and all green beans may be dried after shelling by being spread out in a dry, airy place and stirred occasionally, and are quite different in flavor from dry, ripened beans.

String Beans—Cook beans until half done; drain, dry in sun, pack in paper bags, keep in cool place. To cook—soak over night, cook shorter time than usual.

Mushrooms—String mushroom caps, also stems, on a cord the same as apples, for drying, hang in sun and wind until just before the dew begins to fall and finish drying over the stove, or, dry entirely over the stove.

Put into dry, close covered jars or thick paper sacks. (May wrap in waxed paper before putting into sacks). Keep in dry place.

When first dried, mushrooms may be pulverized in a mortar and the powder put into clean, dry jars. It is delightful for flavoring soups and sauces.

String Beans in Brine

Put layer of salt 1 in. deep in bottom of stone jar or cask; then a layer of nice, tender string beans 3 in. deep; continue layers until cask is full. Cover beans with a board a little smaller around than the inside of the cask or jar and put a heavy stone on it so that the beans will be well covered with the brine. The beans may be put in at different times, but must be covered with the board from the first.

To Cook—Soak over night in cold water, changing the water several times in the early part of the evening. Cook the same as fresh beans, changing the water once or twice while cooking.

They are as nice and fresh as when picked.

Corn in Brine

Put layers of fresh picked corn, cut from the cob, in crock the same as string beans except that the layers of corn should be 1 to 2 in. deep only, and salt ½ in. deep. Have the top layer of salt, and thicker than the others and keep the corn well under the brine with a board and stone.

SOUPS

"The more liquid there is taken into the stomach with the meals, the more difficult it is for the food to digest, for the liquid must first be absorbed."

Consequently, the most perfect hygiene in the use of soups, would call for a few sips only, at the beginning of the meal, which in some cases stimulates the flow of the digestive juices.

With a hearty dinner of other foods, a small portion of some light soup or broth should be served, while a legume soup a chowder or a purée may make the principal dish of the meal.

We seldom make a soup after a recipe. When we serve soups every day, we purposely cook more than is required for other dishes of such things as will make good ingredients for soups; or, if used occasionally only, we make soup at a time when there are left-overs that are suitable. We get better results from these combinations, both from the variety of flavors, and because, with few exceptions, reheating develops richer flavors in foods.

"Our Famous Soups" are some that we have made, at different times, after this plan.

Under the head of soups are classed, bouillons or consommés, bisques, purées and chowders; though some of them are not soups in the strictest sense. For instance, a chowder is often made of the consistency of a stew, with a small proportion of liquid, and, as Francatelli says, "a purée is a kind of pulpy maceration of legumes, vegetables, etc., which have been passed through a fine colander," but both of these are sometimes made with a larger proportion of liquid and served as thick soups.

The word "bisque" means rich soup, so in using it we do not say "tomato bisque soup" because the word soup is comprehended in bisque.

Bouillons (*boo-yon´* or *bool-yon´*) or consommés are broths.

Suggestions

Do not put everything through the colander, (celery and oyster plant, never). Mastication in connection with soups is an aid to their digestion as well as being more satisfying.

Use potatoes seldom in any but potato soups; potato water, not at all. The addition of potatoes to an otherwise wholesome soup might convert it into a fermentable combination: as well as to remove it from the dietary of those who cannot use starchy foods.

Cook turnips and carrots by themselves and drain before adding to soups. The flavor of turnip in soup is often disagreeable.

Utilize the food cutter in preparing vegetables for soups.

As a rule, use oyster plant in slices, ¼ in. thick in the largest part and a little thicker toward the end; but if desired fine, grind it before cooking. In this way it retains its characteristic flavor.

Often the best way to thicken a soup is to heat the flour in oil or butter (without browning) and add some of the hot soup to it as for gravy, so avoiding a scorched taste.

Dried mushrooms washed well, soaked 2 to 4 hours, simmered 5 m., cut fine and added, with their juice, give a fine flavor to many soups. Three or four small pieces are sufficient for 1½ to 2 qts. of soup.

Always keep a quantity of consommé or bouillon on hand, for soups or sauces, or to pour over hash, or chopped potatoes, or to moisten roasts.

Serve bouillon or consommé in cups with or without the beaten white of egg in teaspoonfuls on each.

Whipped cream may be added to bouillon just before serving or dropped by teaspoonfuls on the cups, with a leaf of parsley laid on each.

When soups are lacking in character, the addition of water and salt will develop a meaty flavor, relieving the "porridgy" taste.

Raw nut butter may be added to any of the combinations of vegetables in the proportion of 1 or 1½ tablespns. to each quart of soup.

The water drained from boiled peanuts may be used in place of raw nut butter, taking care not to use too much.

If you should have the thick nut stock, use not more than 2 tablespns. to each quart of soup.

Use herbs sparingly, some, such as mint and thyme, in minute quantities.

In putting corn through a colander, first crush the kernels in a pan or grind them through a food cutter, and put a very little into the colander at a time.

Use poor or top parts of stalks of celery, crushed, for flavoring soups.

Okra is a valuable addition to some soups, tomato soups especially. When using it, take about ¼ less water for the soup, and add from ¼–½ of a pint can to each pint of soup. Heat carefully and serve at once.

The water from spinach is an invaluable addition to vegetable soups, and with the addition of a little cream it alone makes a delightful broth. The water from nearly all greens is desirable in soups.

A little stewed asparagus adds very much to any vegetable soup or chowder.

If soup has thickened by standing, add water or milk before serving.

WATER SOUPS

★ Nut Bouillon

1½ tablespn. raw nut butter

3–4 tablespns. chopped onion

½ cup strained tomato

2–3½ teaspns. browned flour

1–1¼ teaspn. salt

1 qt. water

Rub the nut butter smooth with part of the water, simmer all ingredients together 1½–2 hrs., strain vegetables out, add water to make 1¼ qt., heat, serve.

To Clear—Add water for one quart only, cool, beat with the white and shell of one egg, set over a slow fire and stir often until the broth boils rapidly, then boil without stirring until it looks dark and clear below the scum. Let stand off the fire about 10 m., strain through 2 or 3 thicknesses of cheese cloth laid over a colander; pour through wire strainer on to the cheese cloth. Add more water if necessary after straining, to develop a meaty flavor. Reheat, serve.

★ Vegetable Consommé

With or without 2–3 tablespns. raw nut butter or soup stock.

1–2 large onions, sliced

¼ cup dried celery tops pressed down

2 large bay leaves

2 large tomatoes or ½–⅔ cup stewed tomato

¼ level teaspn. thyme

1 level tablespn. browned flour

2–3 cloves garlic, if desired

2½–3 teaspns. salt

2 qts. water

Cook together 1–2 hours, strain, add water to make 2 quarts, more salt if necessary, heat, serve.

★ Vegetable Consommé, No. 2

Omit browned flour and garlic in preceding recipe, substitute celery salt for celery tops, and add a trifle of sage.

White Stock

- ¼ cup raw nut butter or meal
- 1 large onion, sliced
- 1½ level teaspn. celery salt or seed
- ¼ level teaspn. powdered sage
- ⅛ level teaspn. thyme
- 1 medium bay leaf
- 1½–2 teaspns. salt
- 2–3 qts. water

Mix dry ingredients, add nut butter which has been stirred with water, simmer all together 1½–2 hours, strain, and add water to make 2½ pints, heat, serve.

Dark Stock

- ¼ cup raw nut butter or meal
- 1 medium bay leaf
- 1 level teaspn. celery salt
- ½ level teaspn. powdered sage
- ¼ level teaspn. thyme

1 level tablespn. salt

1 level tablespn. browned flour

1 cup sliced onion

1 clove garlic

2½ qts. water

½ cup strained tomato

Finish the same as white stock, leaving 2½ pts. of stock.

Vegetable Stock

¼ cup each beans and split peas

1 each medium onion and carrot, sliced

1 stalk celery or ¼ cup celery tops or ¼ teaspn. celery seed or salt

1–2 tablespns. chopped parsley

⅛ level teaspn. thyme

½ level teaspn. leaf sage or ¼ powdered

Salt

Simmer all together 3–4 hours; strain, serve. Parsley may be added after straining soup. Savory, marjoram and other herbs may be used, or the herbs may be omitted altogether.

Other legumes may be substituted for the ones given. Tomato or browned flour or both may be added. This stock is excellent for gravies and sauces. A thick soup may be made by rubbing the vegetables through the colander instead of straining them out.

★ Cereal Bouillon

2½ pts. nice fresh bran pressed down. 2½ qts. boiling water. Simmer together 2 hours or more; strain, add

1 pint strained tomato
1 bunch celery stalks, crushed
1 large onion, sliced
¼ teaspn. powdered mint in a muslin bag

Simmer together ½–1 hour, strain, salt to taste, heat, serve. This should make 2½ qts. of soup. Other flavorings maybe used.

In using the bran put up in packages, sift it and use only the coarse part.

Tomato Broth

1 qt. stewed tomato
1 onion, sliced
1 bay leaf
salt
1 pt. water

Simmer all together about 20 m., strain and add water for 1½ qt. of broth. Use plenty of salt. This broth may be cleared the same as bouillon, leaving 1 qt. only. 3 or 4 teaspoons of browned flour may be used.

Legume Broths

Cook beans, lentils or whole green peas, until the water looks rich, but not until the skins begin to break. Strain, making 1 pt. of broth from each pint of legumes. (The legumes remaining may be used for stews and soups). Add salt, heat and serve. These broths are very satisfying. They may be varied by adding different flavorings to legumes while cooking or to broths after straining. Tomato, celery, onion with or without browned flour, or thyme are suitable. Brown beans with onion have quite a different flavor from white beans with onion.

★ Nut French Soup

2 tablespns. raw nut butter
2 cups stewed tomato
6 cups water
½ tablespn. browned flour
½ large onion, sliced
1 large bay leaf
¼ teaspn. powdered sage
¼ teaspn. thyme
2½–3 teaspns. salt

Simmer ½–1 hour, strain, reheat, serve. An English woman in sampling this soup after I had made it up, remarked that it tasted like some of the French soups, hence its name.

Egg Soup

Add salt and butter to water, break eggs into a cup, one for each cup of water, leave whole and turn slowly into the rapidly boiling water, beating briskly with fork or wire whip until the egg is in white and yellow shreds. Boil up well and serve with crackers and celery. This is an emergency soup. Cream may be added to the water instead of butter, or part milk may be used.

★ Nut and Barley Soup

4 tablespns. raw nut butter

2 qts. water

2½ tablespns. coarse pearl barley

½ bay leaf

2 small sticks celery, or a few celery tops

2½–3 teaspns. salt

Cook barley and nut butter in part of the water for 3–5 hours. Add water to make 2 qts., with celery and bay leaf. Simmer from 15–20 m., no longer. Remove celery and bay leaf, serve. Bay leaf may be omitted.

★ Cabbage and Tomato Soup

Cook chopped or finely-shredded cabbage in boiling salted water until tender; add stewed tomatoes, simmer 15–20 m., add necessary salt and water, serve. Excellent.

★ Celery and Tomato Soup

Use stewed celery instead of cabbage in cabbage and tomato soup. A delightful combination.

★ Savory Rice Soup

4 tablespns. raw nut butter

2 qts. water

2½ tablespns. rice

1 teaspn. chopped onion

⅛–¼ teaspn. sage

2½ teaspns. salt

Blend nut butter and water. Heat to boiling, add rice, onion, sage and salt. Boil rapidly until rice is tender.

It may be necessary to add 1–2 cups of water after rice is cooked.

Onion Soup

Simmer sliced onions in butter without browning; add water, boiling, cook until onions are tender, thicken slightly with flour, rub through colander, add salt and a little browned flour, more water if necessary, and chopped parsley.

May cook raw nut butter with onion instead of using dairy butter.

Split Peas and Onion Soup

Split peas, water, salt, raw nut butter and onion, a little tomato sometimes. Cook all ingredients together until peas and onion are tender. Strain or not as preferred.

Potato Soup with Onion or Celery

Simmer chopped onion in oil or butter, add boiling water, potatoes cut in small pieces, and salt. Cook until potatoes are tender, add water to make of the right consistency, salt, and chopped parsley.

Serve with shelled nuts and croutons.

Finely-sliced celery may be cooked with the potatoes, and onions omitted.

Vegetable Soup No. 1

1 cup each carrot, turnip and parsnip in small pieces

2 cups each onion and celery

2 tablespns. raw nut butter

2 qts. boiling water

salt

½ cup rice

Cook all except rice for ½ hour, add rice and cook until it is tender; add 1 tablespn. parsley, more salt and water if necessary.

Vegetable Soup No. 2

Equal quantities carrot and turnip in small pieces, twice as much onion and celery, with raw nut butter and water. Cook until vegetables are tender; add salt and necessary water. In their season, asparagus, peas, and string beans may be added.

Vegetable Soup No. 3

Simmer sliced onions, celery or carrots and cabbage in water, with raw nut butter, until tender. Add browned flour, salt and necessary water; heat.

Mashed legumes may be used in place of nut butter in these vegetable soups. Or they may be made into cream soups by using milk instead of nut butter and water, with or without thickening. Chopped parsley may be used in any of them.

Tomato Soup

1 tablespn. oil or butter

2 tablespns. flour

1 teaspn. salt

1 pt. boiling water

1 qt. stewed tomatoes

Add flour to melted butter in saucepan, pour boiling water over, stirring, add tomatoes and salt. Boil up well.

Chopped onion may be simmered in the oil before adding flour.

Nut Gumbo

3–4 tablespns. raw nut butter

1 2/3 qt. water

2/3 cup nutmese in small oblong pieces

1/3 cup trumese in small oblong pieces

2/3 pt. stewed or canned okra

2/3 cup finely-sliced celery, stewed

1 tablespn. rice, cooked

1/2 tablespn. chopped parsley

salt

Cook raw nut butter in part of the water, add other ingredients, heat well. Cooked noodles may be used instead of rice.

★ Tampa Bay Soup

1 tablespn. oil

1 tablespn. flour

1/2 tablespn. browned flour

1 cup boiling water

1 cup stewed tomato

3 tablespns. raw nut butter

1–1¼ qt. water
½ cup sliced okra
½ cup sliced onion
½ cup trumese in dice
¼ cup nutmese in dice
chopped parsley

Cook tomato, raw nut butter, the 1¼ qt. of water, okra and onion all together, rub through colander and add to sauce made with oil, browned and white flour and the 1 cup of water. Add salt and more water if necessary, and when boiling, the trumese and nutmese, with chopped parsley. Throw egg balls into the soup just before serving, or serve separately in each dish. Or, pass a dish of boiled rice with the soup.

★ Mother's Soup

1 qt. clean wheat bran pressed down in the measure
3 qts. boiling water
2 large onions, sliced or chopped
¼ cup grated carrot
1 bay leaf
1–2 tablespns. browned flour
½ cup chopped turnip
⅛ teaspn. thyme
salt

Cook all except turnip and thyme together 1½–2 hours. About 20 m. before removing from the fire add the turnip, and in 10 m. the thyme; after another 10 m., strain, add salt and more water if necessary, heat.

When soup is boiling rapidly, turn in slowly, in a slender stream, batter for cream noodles, stirring constantly. Boil up well, remove from fire, serve at once.

3–4 tablespns. raw nut butter may be used for stock instead of bran, and 1½ teaspn. lemon juice added when soup is done.

★ Bean Soup

Put the beans into boiling water and cook rapidly until the skins begin to break, then simmer until tender and well dried out. The longer and more slowly the beans are cooked the richer the soup will be. Rub beans through colander, keeping them where they will remain hot during the process. Return to the fire, add boiling water and salt, and simmer for an hour. Stir well and serve.

There are three things essential to the perfection of bean soup: 1st., cook the beans without soaking or parboiling, 2nd., dry out well after they become tender, 3rd., do not let the beans or soup get cold at any time before serving. Warmed-over bean soup is very good, but there is a certain meaty flavor lost by cooling and reheating. Left-overs of bean soup, we usually combine with other ingredients. Brown beans and red make very rich soups, much better than black. One pint of beans will make about 3 qts. of soup.

★ Chick Peas Soup

Make the same as bean soup (except that peas require longer cooking), or cook in consommé. Very rich in flavor.

★ Unstrained Bean Soup

Cook nice tender white beans until partially cooked to pieces. Add salt, and water to make of the right consistency, and simmer slowly ½ hour or longer.

★ Swiss Lentil Soup

1 pint lentils
1 large onion
2–4 tablespns. browned flour
salt

Cook lentils and sliced onion together until lentils are tender and well dried out, rub through colander, add the browned flour and salt, with water to make of the right consistency. (There should be from 2½–3 qts. of soup). Heat ½–1 hour. This makes an unusually meaty-flavored soup.

The idea of combining onion and browned flour with lentils was given me by one who had spent some years among the French in Switzerland.

Swiss Peas or Swiss Bean Soup—May be made the same.

★ Canadian Peas Soup

Cook whole ripe peas with onion and a little garlic, rub through colander, add salt, a little browned flour and powdered sage, with water to make like a broth. Unusually good.

★ Green Peas Soup

Cook green peas until tender, put ¾ of them through the colander, add water and salt, boil up, thicken with a little flour and butter rubbed together, add the whole peas, heat to boiling and serve.

CREAM AND MILK SOUPS

Cream soups do not necessarily contain cream, though the addition of a little improves their flavor.

The simplest ones consist of milk thickened to the consistency of very thin cream, salt, and a vegetable or some other ingredient. If the vegetable is mashed, or is one that does not break to pieces easily, the milk may be added to it, and the whole brought to the boiling point and thickened. In a few exceptional cases the ingredient may be cooked in the milk; nice tender green corn, for instance.

A richer sauce is made by making a roux of 2 level tablespns. of butter, and 1–1½ level tablespn. flour, with a pint of milk, put together in the regular way for sauces; but you will be surprised to see how much better soups (with few exceptions) are without thickening, being free from the porridgy taste of those thickened a trifle too much.

A little cream with the water in which the vegetable was cooked often gives a finer flavored soup than milk and is no more expensive.

Sour cream makes a delightful as well as wholesome substitute for sweet cream in corn, cabbage, tomato, in fact, nearly all vegetable soups.

The following is a list of soups in which the general directions are understood when no exceptions are noted. Salt is understood in all.

★ **Cream of Asparagus**—Cook tougher parts and rub through colander. Throw cooked tips in last unless desired for some other dish. The very toughest parts only make a nice, delicate flavored soup. This is one which favors cream and water instead of milk.

Cream of Bean—Lima, common white, or colored. Cook as for water bean soup, rub through colander or leave in broken pieces. Milk, or cream

★

★

www.ingramcontent.com/pod-product-compliance
Lightning Source LLC
Chambersburg PA
CBHW081120080526
44587CB00021B/3683